Mark Lee

SECURING YOUR PC

In easy steps is an imprint of Computer Step
Southfield Road · Southam
Warwickshire CV47 0FB · United Kingdom
www.ineasysteps.com

Notice of Liability
Every effort has been made to ensure that this book contains accurate
and current information. However, Computer Step and the author
shall not be liable for any loss or damage suffered by readers as a
result of any information contained herein.

Trademarks
Microsoft® and Windows® are registered trademarks of Microsoft
Corporation. All other trademarks are acknowledged as belonging to
their respective companies.

Printed and bound in the United Kingdom

ISBN-13 978-1-84078-336-0
ISBN-10 1-84078-336-2

Contents

1 Introducing PC security 7

PC security is vital 8
The history of PC security 9
Threats to your PC 10
How hackers operate 13
The Vista security model 15
Planning a security strategy 16

2 Physically secure your PC 17

Physical PC security 18
Available options 20
Notebook physical security 23
Further considerations 24

3 People and security 25

The greatest security threat? 26
The Spida worm 27
Password strength 28
Enforcing strong passwords 30

4 Security at startup 31

Security at startup 32
Setting startup passwords 34
Disabling the floppy drive 35

5 Security for users 37

Vista user accounts 38
User account strategies 39
Creating a user account 40
Setting a password 43

Securing your files   45
The Public folder   47
Using local user groups   48
Over-the-shoulder credentials   51
Parental controls   52
Setting time limits   53
Blocking inappropriate content   54

6   The virus threat   55

What is a virus?   56
Installing protection   58
Scanning your PC   60
Are you infected?   61
Preventing virus threats   62
Hoaxes   63
Viruses – think laterally   64

7   Security on the Internet   65

Internet threats   66
Malware   67
Vista Internet security   68
Spyware – educate yourself   69
Windows Defender   70
Antispyware alternatives   73
Internet browsing tips   74
Online banking services   75
Clearing your history   77
Internet certificates   78
Rogue dialers   79
IE security settings   80
IE advanced settings   85
Using the pop-up blocker   86
Turning off auto-complete   88
Disabling add-ons   89
Windows Firewall   90
Testing your security level   95

8   Email security   97

Understanding email security   98
What is phishing?   99

Identifying phishing   100
Dealing with phishing   102
Reporting phishing attempts   103
The Vista phishing filter   104
Marking an email legitimate   105
Junk email   106
Deterring junk email   108
Using an external junk filter   109
Windows Mail junk filter   110
Setting a protection level   111
Adding safe senders   112
Blocking senders   114
More mail security options   116
Using plain text   117
Using rules   118
Testing our message rule   120

9   Securing your network   121

Introducing network security   122
Early considerations   123
Password-protect the router   124
Using a WEP security key   125
Using a WPA security key   126
IP addresses   127
Setting static IP addresses   128
The router firewall   130
Preventing access by time   131
Control by MAC address   133

10   Using policies   135

The Group Policy Editor   136
Getting started   137
Our first policy   139
Securing removable devices   143
Restricting hardware installs   145
Enable administrator access   147
Enable specific device install   148

11   Securing sensitive data   153

What is encryption?   154
Encryption in Vista   155
Other encryption options   156

12   Securing Vista   157

Additional Vista security   158
Disabling services   159
Remote Desktop   160
Windows Explorer   161
File Attributes   162

13   Securing applications   163

Securing your applications   164
Disabling macros   165
Password-protecting files   167

14   Using resources   169

Security resources   170
The Microsoft website   171
Microsoft TechNet   173
Newsgroups   174

15   Disposing of your PC   177

Retiring your PC   178
Preparing to format   179
Formatting the drive   180
Destroying your drive   182

16   Staying protected   183

Computing today   184
Windows Update   185
Using Event Viewer   186

Index   187

1 Introducing PC security

Keeping your PC secure is more important than ever. Understanding why and the threats that exist is the first step towards a secure PC.

8   PC security is vital

9   The history of PC security

10 Threats to your PC

13 How hackers operate

15 The Vista security model

16 Planning a security strategy

PC security is vital

Ask yourself the following questions about your home security:

- Do you leave your doors unlocked at all times, even when out of the house?

- Do you leave large holes and gaps in your fencing?

- Do you leave personal documents and bank account details lying around for anyone to see?

- Would you allow anyone access to your home regardless of who they were, and whether you were in the house or not?

Most people lock their doors when out of the house, keep their fences secure and complete, store their personal documents safely, and take due care when allowing people to enter their home.

Whilst it may seem excessive to compare the security of your PC with the security of your home, and whilst it's good to keep things in perspective, the fact is that both house burglars and criminals hacking into your PC are delighted if they can access your bank account and identity details. Experts report that identity theft is the fastest-growing form of crime, and your PC can prove a lucrative target for criminals. In this light, it's clear to see that securing your PC today really is vital.

The good news

Fortunately, it's not all doom and gloom. The fact that you are reading this book is a good start on the road to a secure PC. With an awareness of PC security issues, the implementation of some essential security measures, and due diligence in monitoring the ongoing security of your machine, you can ensure that your PC will be suitably safe for now and the future.

The cost

There's more good news. Securing your PC need not be expensive. It's certainly cheaper than securing your home! Many of the tools we will be using in this book are available without cost to the personal user (and at minimal cost to the business user), and many other tools are already available within Windows Vista itself, which Microsoft has designed to be a very secure system.

Don't forget

Whilst it's important to take measures towards securing your PC, make sure you don't allow the security threats to spoil your enjoyment and the benefits of modern home computing.

Don't forget

A little effort towards securing your PC can mean peace of mind and the protection of what may be some of the most important information you own.

The history of PC security

We need to protect our PC and its valuable data against today's threats. So why look at the history of PC security?

The changes that have occurred in personal computing can actually teach us a lot about why PC security is so much more important today, and why the scope of threats is so much greater.

Early PCs

When personal computers first became an option for home users, the main concern with securing the computer revolved around the physical security of the machine itself. This meant that to prevent unwanted access to your files, you had to ensure that unauthorized people could not physically use the computer. As modems and networks were rare for home users, the risk of somebody outside of the room accessing your PC remotely was not present.

Viruses at this time were largely spread by floppy disks, and so it was also important to restrict which disks went into your drives.

Windows 3.1

The Windows 3.1 line saw the emergence of some new threats, due to the introduction of improved networking capabilities. Suddenly, the threats could come from another computer on the network as well as the one you were sitting at.

Windows 95 and onwards

Windows 95 made Internet access easy, and whilst the Internet has revolutionized our access to information, our PC can also potentially be accessed by computers on the world's largest network. Since then, securing your PC has become more important.

Don't forget

Physical PC security is still important today, and we will be investigating this topic in chapter 2.

Beware

You still need to be alert to viruses being spread by floppy disks, or any other removable devices, such as CDs or USB flash drives.

Threats to your PC

With a wide range of threats lurking to cause harm to our PC and data, it's a wonder we ever use our computers at all! One of the best ways to begin your journey into securing your PC is to demystify some of the terms and names that are used to describe these threats. Once you know which threats exist and what they do, it's easier to get on with the job of protecting against them.

The actions in this book are intended to protect you against all of the following threats.

Malware
Malware is a general term that refers to any kind of malicious software. This includes viruses, worms, trojan horses, adware, and spyware.

Grayware
Grayware is another general term referring to malicious software, but it does not include viruses. It is a name designed to describe any malicious programs that fall in the "gray" area between viruses and standard programs.

Viruses
A computer virus is a program, usually with malicious intentions, that can make copies of itself and "infect" other machines, in the same way that a human virus infects people.

- Viruses usually have a "payload", which is the action that it takes, such as deleting files, or presenting a message

- Viruses use legitimate files on your machine to run inside

Worms
Worms are similar to viruses, but they use a computer network to "infect" other machines by sending copies of themselves.

- Worms cause computer networks to run more slowly

- Worms can spread at an alarming rate. It has been estimated that the MyDoom worm infected a quarter of a million PCs in one day

- Worms usually carry a payload too

- People often use the term "virus" when describing a worm

Beware

Viruses can change and become more powerful as they move to more machines. Other virus writers often amend existing viruses to increase their danger.

Beware

Look out for worms that arrive as email attachments. A file that may seem to be a document or spreadsheet can be a malicious program in disguise.

Trojan horses

A trojan horse is a (usually) harmful program that can hide within a legitimate application on your machine.

- Trojan horses can "hide" inside existing programs, or disguise themselves as useful applications, such as a "free" screensaver

- The user on the infected machine needs to run a program for the trojan to work

- Trojan horses often allow hackers access to your PC over the network structure of the Internet

Spyware

Spyware programs are installed without the user's consent, for the purpose of collecting information and sending it back to a specified source.

- Spyware is sometimes designed to find bank account details and send these back to another computer

- Spyware is also used to send web browsing information back to advertisers, who can then target users with unsolicited adverts

Adware

Adware is software installed on a PC that automatically displays advertising to the user, usually in the form of "pop-up" windows.

- Adware can also include spyware characteristics and send information back to a remote computer without the user's consent

Junk email, or spam

Just as you receive "junk" mail in your home mailbox, you can also receive junk mail in your computer's email inbox.

- Junk email, often known as "spam", accounts for a large percentage of email on the Internet

- Though seemingly harmless, spam is time-consuming to remove, and clogs up email inboxes. At its most extreme, it has resulted in email servers crashing

Beware

Spyware has even been included in the installation of some quite well known packages. Fortunately, most companies have distanced themselves from spyware now.

Hot tip

Never reply to spam, even if offered an "unsubscribe" option. This confirms an active email address to the spammer and almost invariably results in more spam.

...cont'd

Phishing

Phishing is a method that criminals use to attempt to fraudulently gain personal information from a person. These attempts usually take the form of an email.

● Phishing commonly masquerades as a request from your bank for account details, but can also take the form of a message from a body such as eBay or PayPal

● Phishing techniques use "social engineering" to try to extract personal data from people. Social engineering is the process of manipulating people into telling you their personal information, such as account details or passwords

Hackers

Hackers are people that illegitimately gain access to computers and computer systems. While doing so, they may manipulate or delete data, take information or software, and cause problems on the system they have entered.

● A hacker could be sitting in front of the computer they are trying to "break" into, or they may be hacking from another country thousands of miles away

Direct denial of service (DDoS) attacks

Direct denial of service attacks aim to block communication between computer resources and their users. This usually involves efforts to prevent web servers providing web pages to their visitors.

● DDoS attacks use large numbers of PCs to carry out these coordinated attacks

● Your PC could be used for a DDoS attack without your knowledge

Zombie PCs

A zombie PC is one that is under the control of a hacker or malware program. It could then be used for a DDoS attack, or any number of tasks as the remote hacker chooses.

Rootkits

Rootkits attempt to mask processes from the user and Windows itself, potentially hiding the existence of malicious software.

How hackers operate

Hacking illegitimately into computers is an activity that has been taking place almost as long as computers have existed. Therefore it should be no surprise that the methods that today's hackers use are complex indeed! They have built their skills upon the years of work that have been done before them.

Having an overview of the skills and methods employed by hackers is useful when considering how to protect your PC and its valuable data. Let's have a look at some of the ways hackers try to break into your PC.

Social engineering

Whilst many view the shadowy world of hackers as a collection of highly skilled and intelligent computer experts, the fact is that many hackers are more skilled at manipulating people than manipulating machines.

Hackers use their personality and psychological skills to perform acts such as masquerading as IT staff in order to persuade people to reveal their passwords. Social engineering has been argued to be the most powerful tool in the hacker's toolkit.

Network tools

Network tools are another powerful asset for the hacker. Running a "ping" can tell a hacker if a computer is active on the Internet.

Backdoor and remote-control tools

Some network tools exist that allow hackers to remotely control your PC over a network on the Internet. Whilst these tools often provide valuable support functions for IT staff, they can also be abused by hackers who use this power for malicious and criminal ends. Back Orifice and NetBus are well known examples.

Don't forget

Phishing attempts are a form of social engineering.

Beware

Though some people regard Back Orifice and NetBus as having legitimate uses, most security packages identify them as malicious.

13

Beware

NetBus is easily downloadable by hackers, and Back Orifice is under continual development. You must be vigilant as hackers' tools are constantly evolving.

...cont'd

Beware

In addition to the password stealing methods we've looked at, hackers also use tools that "crack" passwords by looking up dictionary words and using "brute force" to try numerous combinations of characters.

Beware

It's not just network performance that is affected by other people secretly using your wireless connection. They may be using it to surf on illegal websites, and therefore it is vital that you follow the measures in this book to keep them out.

Hot tip

Viruses, worms, and trojan horses may often have different names across different security companies. As with all PC security, it's important to do your research.

Keystroke capture

Often included in remote control tools, as well as being used as tools in themselves, keystroke capture applications catch and record everything typed on a user's keyboard. This can include all information keyed, such as usernames and passwords.

Other programs are able to identify credit card numbers and bank account details within the captured information, and these tools pose a very serious threat indeed.

War driving and piggybacking

Unsecured wireless networks are an easy target for hackers. Offenders drive around an area, equipped with a wireless-enabled notebook, and attempt to locate unsecured wireless systems, reporting the location back to others, usually via a website. At the very least they may attempt to "piggyback" onto the wireless network to gain some free surfing, and at the worst they may hack into the associated PC, or use the free web surfing for criminal and undesirable means.

Viruses, trojan horses, and worms

Whilst viruses initially attempted tasks such as deleting files on a computer's hard drive, criminals have harnessed their power for devious exploits. Trojan horses in particular have been used to "harvest" personal details, including bank account details, usernames, and passwords, from unsuspecting computer users. An example is the M311 trojan horse, described on the Symantec site below as the "Backdoor.Haxdoor" trojan horse.

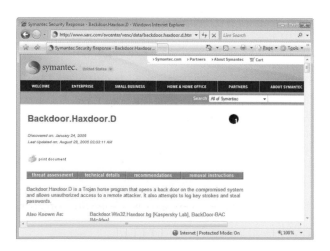

The Vista security model

When Windows Vista was being designed, Bill Gates wanted to ensure that security was a number one consideration, from day one. So Windows Vista includes a number of new security features, including:

- Parental Controls to ensure that children are securely protected on the Internet and restricted where required

- An advanced user account model, known as User Account Control, meaning that users are less likely to inadvertently create or fall victim to security vulnerabilities

- "Over-the-shoulder credentials", where the system administrator can temporarily assign greater powers to the user when required, rather than assigning these powers on a permanent basis

- A phishing filter, designed to recognize phishing attempts, alert the user, and "quarantine" the offending item in a selected folder

- "Windows Defender", an application to detect and alert the user to potentially malicious software before any changes are made to the system

- Advanced features in the Windows Firewall

- "Network Access Protection" to prevent computers from connecting to your private network if they do not meet certain security standards

We'll make sure that we take advantage of Vista's excellent range of security features when securing our PC throughout this book, and taking other measures too where necessary.

A layered approach to PC security

PC security experts advise that you should not regard any single security measure as a "panacea" or "cure-all" for all security risks. They recommend what has become known as a "layered" approach to protecting your PC, in which you incorporate a host of necessary measures to seal off all potential vulnerabilities. In this book, we will be working through the measures required to carefully implement these layers and provide solid protection for your PC and its valuable data.

Don't forget

It is impossible for any software to be totally secure, as a balance needs to be maintained between security and usability. Therefore, no matter how secure Windows Vista is, you still need to take additional security precautions and ensure others follow your good example.

Hot tip

Note that due to the nature of many of the procedures in this book, you will often need to be logged in as an administrator.

Planning a security strategy

To return to our idea of securing your home, you probably have a security strategy of some kind in place. For example:

Don't forget

As we've discussed, the information held on your computer may be some of the most important property you own, so PC security is almost as vital as home security.

- Lock the doors when leaving the house

- Set the burglar alarm

- Close off any gaps or "weak points" in the fencing around your home

- Store any precious goods or possessions in secure and obscure locations

As you make your way through this book, and as you learn more about securing your PC, it's a good idea to build a clear security strategy, and then implement it.

We've learned some skills to put to work in our strategy already, such as:

Hot tip

It is very important to keep your security strategy safe from prying eyes, to prevent your privacy and data from being compromised. We'll be looking at securing your documents with passwords later in the book. Your security strategy will be one of the very documents you need to protect in this way.

- Don't reply to spam emails

- Never give out your password or bank account details to anyone

- Be careful with which programs and applications you choose to run

Consider placing your thoughts in a document, and then keep it in a safe place.

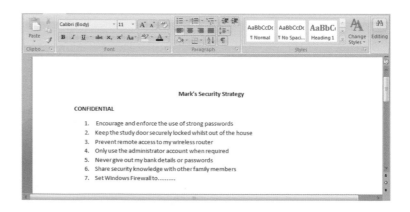

2 Physically secure your PC

It's often the most overlooked factor, but the physical security of your PC is vital.

18 Physical PC security

20 Available options

23 Notebook physical security

24 Further considerations

Physical PC security

It's great news for people today that modern PCs are not only powerful, highly functional, and easy to use, but also cheaper than ever before.

It's perhaps because of this reduced value that people often overlook the physical security issues surrounding their PC. What's important to consider is not so much the value of your PC, but rather the value of the information stored on your PC.

Modern PCs hold valuable information

Take a moment to think about the sorts of information you store on your PC:

- Personal documents including letters?
- Personal finance information?
- Your children's homework?
- Family photographs?
- Business accounts or other information?
- Copies of your website information?

It's likely that you will store some, if not all, of the above information, and maybe more besides.

Now ask yourself if you use any of the following services:

- Online banking services?
- Online stores?
- Other online services?

Your information is more valuable than your PC

With the range of confidential and valuable information being stored on and exchanged via a personal computer nowadays, such as that listed above, this data is almost invariably of greater value than the actual hardware itself. Therefore, you have to consider the real price of failing to physically secure your PC.

To really appreciate why our PC data is more valuable than our PC, we need to understand what criminals want from a stolen computer.

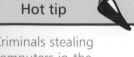

Hot tip

Criminals stealing computers in the eighties and nineties were mainly interested in selling the hardware for profit. Modern computer thieves are much more likely to be looking at stealing the information inside.

18

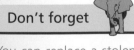

Don't forget

You can replace a stolen PC. Can you replace your stolen data?

What do criminals want from your PC?

Having your PC stolen would be painful enough. Losing stored digital photographs, college documents, and locally stored email correspondence would make matters even worse. Criminals, though, are looking to get their hands on other information inside your computer, such as that mentioned on the previous page.

The most valuable prizes for computer thieves are bank account details and other financial data. As we will be noting throughout this book, criminals desperately want your banking information and other personal details to exploit for financial theft, identity fraud, resale to other criminals, and other devious uses. By this token it is essential that you thwart them by closing down as many vulnerabilities as you can, and one of the primary elements you must address is that of the physical security of your machine.

The first steps of physical PC security

Let's start taking some steps towards ensuring the physical security of your PC, by considering home security.

1. Is your computer visible from the outside of your home? As with all valuable possessions, be sure to locate it away from direct viewing where possible, whether through windows, or doors if fitted with glass

2. Consider fitting internal locks. Burglars are frustrated by locked internal doors, which greatly hinder their progress, and if your computer is located in a locked room, they may struggle to access it, or not even try to break in at all

3. Try to avoid giving "clues" as to where your PC is located. For instance, when you're using that large, glowing, flat-panel monitor late at night, close the blinds or curtains to avoid advertizing your wares to any criminal elements

4. Any increased security to your home is good news for your PC security. Remember that the majority of burglaries involve criminals targeting properties from brief scans of people's homes, so visual deterrents such as alarms, heavy door locks, and secure windows pay dividends in the long term

Beware

The total cost of your PC will most likely be lower than the price you could pay as a victim of identity theft.

Hot tip

If the unthinkable happens and your PC is stolen, contact your bank immediately if you have used online banking services on the PC.

Beware

If you are securing a PC for your own business, be aware that increased responsibility is on your shoulders, and you may have some legal responsibilities to honor. This will be particularly pertinent if you process and store customer information.

20

Beware

It's a hard fact to face, but if your PC is stolen, there's a chance that, given time, the criminals will be able to access your data, and possibly your browsing history, too. Follow the steps in this book to help make their job more difficult.

Don't forget

With regards to PC security, prevention is invariably better than cure. Keep your PC secure and safe out of sight and reach of potential intruders.

Available options

After you've considered and taken action on any of the applicable preliminary steps we've outlined towards physical PC security, you need to begin thinking about other options available to you.

The other options you choose should reflect a balance between:

- The "value" of the information stored on your computer

- The cost of the security you select

If your computer is only used for, say, playing games and listening to music, then the price you pay for security measures should be fairly moderate.

If, on the other hand, you use your PC for online banking, home finances, business work, building your website, and other high-sensitivity tasks, then you would want to consider spending considerably more on physical security measures.

Keep the value of your data in mind when choosing how much to spend on physical PC security.

Physical security measures on offer

OK, now that we've established the importance of physical PC security and how we should balance the measures taken with the value of what we might lose, let's browse through some of the options available, using some examples you can find online.

Cables

Perhaps the most cost-effective physical PC security measure is to invest in a security cable.

Security cables work by looping through attachments you glue onto the PC and chosen peripherals, such as your monitor or printer. Some PC manufacturers sell their computers with attachments already integrated into the case, which makes for a very secure solution.

If possible, it is worth channeling the security cable through your office desk, to further deter and prevent the risk of theft.

Check the specification of any cable you consider purchasing, to assess how difficult it may be for a burglar to remove it.

There are many cable options on the market for you to choose from, such as this one at www.secure-it.com:

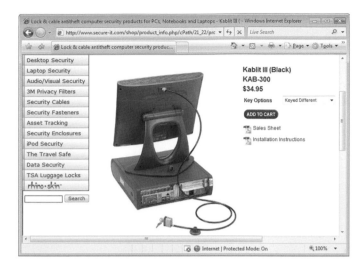

Don't forget

Keep the keys to your security devices safe. You don't want to secure your computer against yourself!

Cages

Security cables help to prevent a thief from stealing your PC base unit, but they may leave some opportunity for the individual to force access inside the PC and steal the hard drive. If it is your information that they wish to steal, this may be as valuable a prize for them as stealing the whole computer, and much lighter for them to transport away from the site.

To take a step up the security ladder, you may wish to consider a cage (also sometimes known as a "clamp"). These are made of toughened metal, and "wrap" around the base unit. They can usually be bolted to the floor.

The main advantage with a cage is that it virtually eliminates access to the insides of the PC, and thus prevents access to your hard drive and the precious data stored within. This example is from www. compucage.com:

Hot tip

PC manufacturers that integrate loops in their PC cases for security cables tend to design these so that the presence of the cable restricts case opening. This is preferable to the situation with standard cases, where you need to glue attachments for the cable to the case.

21

Don't forget

Strong PC security involves the "layered" approach. No single security measure is enough to provide quality security, but implementing complementary measures will mean that your PC is protected from a multitude of threats.

Enclosures

PC cages or clamps provide a definite security hike. However, they may still leave physical vulnerabilities in the form of access to drives and ports, where criminals could choose to use floppy disks or USB flash drives to attempt to steal your information.

Full PC enclosures represent the highest level of physical PC security. These units remove all external access to the PC base unit by enclosing the unit in a lockable case. Have a look at the example shown from www.pcguard.co.uk.

Floppy drive locks

If you don't want to pay the price for a full enclosure, which may be quite expensive, but are willing to purchase a cage or clamp, you can prevent access to the floppy drive using a drive lock, like the example pictured from computersecurity.com.

Tracking devices

If your PC holds extremely confidential or "mission critical" information, you may want to consider a tracking device. Computer tracking devices function by "hiding" on your PC and then surreptitiously emailing the security company if stolen and reattached to an Internet connection. The security company can then aim to "track" and recover the PC by tracing the phone number used to dial out.

This type of system does have limitations. It is not effective if the PC is "wiped", or if the hard drive is replaced by the criminals before the computer is sold on, and you need to check if the system relies on a certain connection type being used (telephone dial-up, for instance) to be effective.

Notebook physical security

With continual improvements in design and technology, Notebooks have evolved to their current state of being lightweight, portable, and inconspicuous. Whilst this is a clear benefit to commuting business people and those on the move, it also makes the notebook an appealing target for criminals, so let's look at some physical security options specifically for notebooks.

Cables

Virtually all modern notebooks come with a special slot known as a "Kensington security slot" (also known as a K-slot) that you can attach security cables to. Attach the cable when you set your notebook up on the desk, and lock it with the key, which you must remember to take with you if you leave your desk! Here's an example from the www. kensington.com website:

Alarm

Some notebook security companies offer notebook alarms. You can set these when you leave your notebook, and any attempt to move your notebook or remove the device triggers a loud alarm.

Notebook lockers

Custom-sized lockers can be fitted to desks for secure storage of notebooks. You could also attach them to the inside of cupboards or wardrobes in the home for less conspicuous notebook storage. Some models offer a small opening at the rear for easy charging, such as this one from www. wedgwood-group.com.

Hot tip

The company Kensington designed the Kensington security slot, and whilst they manufacture cables to attach to the slot, other manufacturers also supply cable products that comply to the standard and are hence usable with the slot. Notebook and cable manufacturers should use the Kensington "K" padlock logo for easy identification of compatibility with the design.

Hot tip

Many notebook alarms also use the Kensington slot.

Beware

Notebook alarms are only really useful when you are within close proximity of the notebook. It's not an effective prevention for all situations and requires complementary security measures, such as a secure cable.

Further considerations

If you've opted for some of the physical security measures we've looked at so far for your PC or notebook, then your computer should have made some progress up the security ladder.

There are still some other options and considerations that you may wish to think about.

Let's start by mentioning a couple of quick and easy options that weren't covered previously.

- "Invisible ink" pens can be used to write your area code details onto the PC or notebook case. Invisible to the naked eye, the ink can be viewed under ultraviolet light, and may assist the police in identifying your machine if recovered

- Some companies offer to "stamp" your PC case or provide adhesive labels that leave an indelible mark on the machine if removed. This is a clear deterrent to thieves and spoils their opportunities for resale

Storage

Just as it's easy to overlook the importance of physically securing your PC, there are other elements that are even further down people's security lists. The issue of storage is perhaps the most significant of these.

- Your backup media. Whether you back up to CD, DVD, external hard drive, USB flash drive or another device, leaving criminals with access to your backup media is almost as good as handing them your hard drive. Your backups will contain your most vital data, so you should keep them stored safely

- Your software. Original software CDs are a valuable commodity to criminals. Keep them locked away safely

- Whilst delightfully easy to use, USB flash drives present a real security problem. Don't leave them dangling out of your computer while unattended, or lying on the desk. Store them away safely

Think like a criminal!

Difficult though it may be, remember to think like a criminal when assessing your physical PC security needs, and plug all vulnerabilities accordingly. Remain vigilant and flexible!

Don't forget

There's little point in spending out on maximum security measures for your PC if you leave your backup media with all of your valuable data in easy reach!

Hot tip

We'll be looking at other measures to protect you against the security threats posed by USB flash drives later in the book.

24

3 People and security

Beware! One of the greatest security threats to your PC is the innocent user.

26 The greatest security threat?

27 The Spida worm

28 Password strength

30 Enforcing strong passwords

The greatest security threat?

It is an unfortunate fact that many well-meaning PC users are inadvertently responsible for the most serious security problems on your PC. Whether it's your nephew downloading Internet games, or your partner submitting your bank details to a malicious source, the innocent user can unwittingly become the greatest security threat to your PC and its valuable data.

Security threats introduced by people using your PC can include:

- Easy access to documents and other files through the use of inadequate passwords

- The download and installation of malicious programs from the Internet

- Disclosure of bank details or other important information

- Easier access to your PC by remote hackers

- Access to important and sensitive documents stored on portable storage devices, such as USB flash drives

- Creating holes in your network security by installing new hardware or services without adequate protection being configured

- Access to browsing information and history

This list is not exhaustive, and you need to be vigilant in identifying potential new threats.

Educate yourself, then educate others

Whilst it's important to keep your PC security concerns in perspective, you do need to stay on top of the evolution and emergence of new threats. Educate yourself by reading media articles, websites, forums, message boards, and any other sources you find useful.

Keeping on top of PC security concerns is certainly good practice, but the benefits of this approach are reduced if other users of your PC are unaware of potential risks and pitfalls. Whilst they may not need to maintain the same amount of security knowledge as you, it's sensible to pass down the main elements to them.

Don't forget

Security threats come in many different forms, and are continually evolving.

Hot tip

Communicate your security ideas and knowledge to others who use your PC.

Hot tip

Why not create a checksheet for other users of your PC, providing security guidelines and reminders?

26

The Spida worm

A lack of good practice in computer security can be seen at many different levels. Even corporate IT departments can fail to implement the required level of security in today's computing environment.

An illustration of this occurred back in May 2002, when the "Spida" worm spread rapidly across servers, infecting a reported 10,000 machines during the first month alone. The worm wreaked havoc with computer systems and attempted to send sensitive information back to a specific computer.

The Spida worm carried out its malicious processes not through some complex password-finding programming, but rather by working upon the assumption that IT system administrators would have used blank passwords on specific types of server.

Whilst it seems unlikely that this approach would have yielded many victims, the fact that 10,000 machines were infected inside a month reveals how vital good-quality security is.

If you want to read about how the Spida worm worked, try searching on an antivirus software site, such as www.nai.com.

Don't forget

Even IT professionals make security oversights sometimes!

Hot tip

Learn about specific viruses and how they operate to better protect yourself against them.

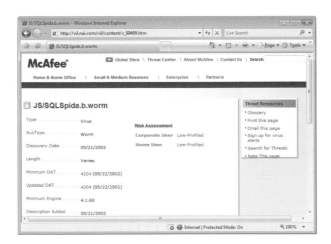

The Spida worm outbreak is important because it tells us:

- Poor computer security can have large consequences

- Good-quality passwords are essential

Password strength

As we have seen, the Spida worm took advantage of poor password management. It is essential that you:

- Resist the temptation to leave passwords blank
- Use passwords that are of sufficient strength

What makes a weak password?

Before outlining what makes a strong password, it's useful to analyze the characteristics of a weak password.

A weak password can be characterized by any of a number of attributes, including:

- Inadequate length
- Being easily guessable
- Using a common word
- Variations of the username
- Using the default password
- People's names
- Meaningful dates, such as the user's date of birth

Remember that cases of social engineering can involve malicious individuals discovering personal information about others, and then exploiting this information to guess their passwords. Beware of any suspicious sources trying to find out this information from you, and avoid using personal information in your passwords.

Examples of weak passwords

Examples of weak passwords include:

- password
- 01/12/74
- september02
- nicole
- car
- johnsmith1234

Don't forget

You need to ensure that other users of your PC are also using strong passwords, to ensure security is not compromised.

Beware

Some hackers or viruses use dictionary attacks, so even words you consider obscure may not be strong enough.

Beware

Social engineering can come in unexpected forms, such as online surveys.

... cont'd

In order to minimize the risk of passwords being guessed or discovered, you need to ensure that you integrate some elements to make this more difficult.

What makes a strong password?

Strong passwords can be characterized by the inclusion of attributes such as:

- Greater length

- The use of both lower- and upper-case characters

- Combining letters and numbers

- The use of symbols, such as a question mark, or an exclamation mark

- Using seemingly random combinations of characters

- Avoiding inclusion of the username

Examples of strong passwords

Examples of strong passwords include:

- nYt7Hbbv98i

- !ng78FGDhD88@*&

Creating memorable strong passwords

The two examples above, whilst very strong, are clearly not very memorable, which could cause you further problems. In order to remember strong passwords, consider using combinations of letters, numbers and symbols which are meaningful to you but not others.

As an example, consider:

- iNe@SyS&eP$

Whilst seemingly random, it is based upon the three words "ineasysteps", with certain letters replaced by symbols, and variations of upper and lower case. You can also incorporate numbers if you wish, for example by replacing the letter "O" with the number "0" (zero).

Hot tip

It's possible that not all systems will allow the use of all types of symbols in passwords.

Beware

Whilst more secure, setting password strength requirements too high can be counterproductive, with people writing down complex passwords to remind themselves of them. These passwords are subsequently easier for malicious individuals to find and abuse.

Enforcing strong passwords

In Windows Vista, Microsoft has provided a method of ensuring that all users of your PC choose Windows passwords of sufficient strength. You will need to be logged in as an administrator to be able to run this process.

1 Click on the Start button, and then Control Panel

2 Double-click Administrative Tools, then Local Security Policy. A warning window will appear. This is User Account Control asking us to authorize a change to our system. As we have invoked the change, click Continue

3 Vista will present you with the Local Security Settings window. In the left pane, double-click Account Policies, and then click Password Policy

4 Double-click "Password must meet complexity requirements", then select the Enabled radio button. Click OK, and close all windows to finish

4 Security at startup

Security should start before

Windows is even launched.

32 Security at startup

34 Setting startup passwords

35 Disabling the floppy drive

Security at startup

It is vital to secure Windows against the raft of threats, vulnerabilities and security risks existing in today's computing environment. Yet there are further security measures you can implement that take effect before Windows is even launched.

The BIOS

Personal computers and notebooks contain a set of programming code that runs before Windows launches. This is known as the BIOS. The BIOS prepares the computer so that Windows can "talk" to the installed hardware. It also contains some features that can be used to secure your PC.

A warning about the BIOS

Implementing BIOS security is a good complementary measure for your overall PC security strategy. However, you need to be aware of an inherent weakness in using the BIOS as a security method. The BIOS "remembers" its settings using a small battery located inside your PC, known as the CMOS battery. For a malicious individual to reset your BIOS settings, they can open your machine, remove the battery, allow it to drain, and then reinsert it again. The BIOS will return to its default settings, and your security settings will be lost. Therefore, it is an important step to physically secure your computer, as we examined in chapter 2.

Entering the BIOS

Different hardware manufacturers use different versions of BIOS, but they all share common features. For the purposes of the following examples, we are going to use the Phoenix-Award-style BIOS, but your computer manual or manufacturer website should be able to give you instructions on how to use your particular type.

Let's see how we can enter the BIOS startup options.

1. Power on your PC using the power button

2. The screen will display a message telling you which keys to press to enter your BIOS options. For our Phoenix-Award BIOS, we need to press the Delete key

32

3 The BIOS settings screen should appear, with a host of options to choose from

4 Don't make any changes yet! We'll be looking at how to implement security features in the BIOS shortly. If you don't wish to move on to those steps yet, press the Escape key, and select Y to quit without saving

```
Quit Without Saving <Y/N>? N
```

Keystrokes used to enter the BIOS setup

There are many different keystrokes used to enter the BIOS, depending upon which company manufactured your specific BIOS type. There will usually be a brief message on the screen informing you of what to press, although some manufacturers hide this message to prevent accidental changes. If you don't see a message, consult your PC or system-board manual.

Some common keystrokes used to enter BIOS setup utilities include:

- The Delete key

- The Escape key

- The F1, F2 or F10 keys

- Ctrl and Alt plus the Escape key

- Ctrl and Alt plus the Delete key

Beware

Always take care when using your computer's BIOS. It is possible to cause damage to your system if you select the incorrect options.

33

Setting startup passwords

There are two types of startup password you can set on your machine, allowing different types of access. A Supervisor password protects access to the BIOS utility, whereas a User password provides password protection for when the PC boots up.

The Supervisor password
The Supervisor password protects the BIOS utility by restricting access only to those who know the password. Let's set a Supervisor password in the Award-type BIOS.

1 Enter your BIOS utility by pressing the appropriate keys

2 At the main BIOS screen, use the arrow keys to select the Set Supervisor Password option and press Enter

3 Key in a password, press Enter, and key in the same password again, pressing Enter to confirm

4 Press F10, and then Y when asked to save. Press Enter to confirm and the PC will reboot. The Supervisor password is set

Disabling the floppy drive

Floppy disk drives are seldom used on computers nowadays, but they still present a risk to security. They can introduce viruses and other malware, and they can be used for the theft of information from your computer.

Do you really still need to use your floppy drive? If not, let's look at two options for disabling floppy drive access.

Disable the floppy drive in the BIOS

Disabling the floppy drive in the BIOS has limitations, but is still a useful step to take.

1 Enter the BIOS setup utility according to your particular type. We're using the Phoenix-Award type again, but remember that settings will vary according to the BIOS type in your PC

2 Press the down-arrow key until the Integrated Peripherals option is highlighted, then press Enter

3 Use the down-arrow key to move to the Onboard FDC Controller option

...cont'd

4 Press Enter, and then use the up- or down-arrow keys to select the Disabled option. If it is different in your BIOS version, carefully look for references to the FDC, as this is the floppy disk controller

5 Press Enter to confirm the change, and then F10 to exit, pressing Y when asked if you are sure

Remove the floppy drive

Changing the startup settings to disable the floppy drive is a good step to take, but remember that the BIOS is vulnerable to a determined individual, who can adjust the settings if they manage to remove the internal CMOS battery.

For a more secure method of disabling the floppy disk, consider disconnecting the drive cable, or removing the drive completely.

If you are comfortable with performing basic hardware maintenance on your PC, follow these steps.

1 Remove power to your PC, and open the case so that you have access to your system board

2 Locate the ribbon cable that links the floppy disk drive to the system board. This should be marked on the system board as the FDC socket

3 Carefully remove this cable from both the floppy drive and the system board, and store it away. Close the case and replace power to the system

If you are unsure about the process, consult a qualified engineer, and request that the FDC cable be unplugged and removed.

Don't forget

Always contact a qualified PC engineer if you are unsure about performing hardware maintenance tasks.

5 Security for users

Do you want all users of your PC to have the same access? Can everyone access all files as they please? Should children be able to access any web content at any time? If the answer to those questions is "no", you need to implement user security.

38 Vista user accounts

39 User account strategies

40 Creating a user account

43 Setting a password

45 Securing your files

47 The Public folder

48 Using local user groups

51 Over-the-shoulder credentials

52 Parental controls

53 Setting time limits

54 Block inappropriate content

Vista user accounts

If you were running a business, would you allow everybody to access all information within your company, regardless of its sensitivity? Could the marketing department have access to everyone's payroll data, and should the sales team be able to log on and work with the information held by the IT department?

Of course, most businesses take measures to secure data in a way that means only the intended people can work with specific information. Whereas this used to be a case of storing locked filing cabinets in different departments, a large amount of information is now stored electronically, and IT system administration to secure this data accordingly is a full time job.

At home

Just as providing different access to different people and groups is vital in business, you will want to implement some level of access control, albeit on a different scale, on your home PC. The level of control that you implement will depend upon how many people use your PC at home, and how much control and access to information you want them to have.

Windows Vista user account model

In early incarnations of Windows, user profiles were used less for security purposes, and more for retaining different settings for different PC users. The PC log-on screen was easily avoided by cancelling the log-on process, and access was then available to the files on the machine. As Windows has become more advanced, user profiles have come to lend users more security, and with Windows Vista, they are offered the best security options so far:

- "User Account Control" means that all users run at a standard, safe level

- If users need to perform a potentially damaging task, an administrator can use "over-the-shoulder" credentials to temporarily allocate them sufficient rights to complete the task

- Even administrators run at the standard level, and are warned if they are about to make a potentially damaging change

- PC owners can continue to secure data on the machine by user profile as in earlier Windows versions

Hot tip

An administrator is a user who has elevated rights to a computer and its data.

Hot tip

With all users launching programs in standard mode, the opportunity for malware to cause problems is vastly reduced.

User account strategies

In chapter 1, we looked at the idea of developing a security strategy for our PC. Consider spending some time on creating the user account section of your document.

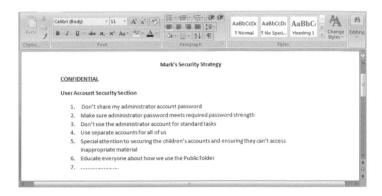

For your security strategy, you need to incorporate the following elements, amongst any other ideas you may have:

● Do not share the administrator account password with anyone

● Ensure the administrator account password meets password strength requirements, as discussed in chapter 3

● Don't log on with the administrator account to perform standard tasks: create a separate, standard user account for yourself

● Create a separate account for each user of the machine

● Disable the "Guest" account

● Educate others as to what should and shouldn't be stored in the "Public" folder

● Ensure that the children have parental controls applied as appropriate

● Remember to apply security to files that you may want others to be able to read, but not modify

We'll be exploring how to achieve all of these tasks throughout the chapter.

Creating a user account

We've explored why it is a good idea to have different user accounts for different users, rather than using one account for everyone. Windows Vista is a secure operating system, and it will only allow people to log on if they have a user account on the PC.

Let's create a standard user account. You need to be logged in as an administrator. Vista will have walked you through creating an administrator profile when you first set up your computer.

Hot tip

It's best to have just one administrator account on your PC. The more administrator accounts you use, the greater the chances are of somebody abusing one of them.

Hot tip

Notice the shield icon next to some of the options, including our "Manage another account" option. The shield indicates that you will need administrator rights to run the option.

40

1 Click Start, and Control Panel

2 Double-click the User Accounts icon

3 At the User Accounts window, click "Manage another account"

4 Notice that the screen darkens and a User Account Control warning appears. This is User Account Control in action! Even though we are logged in as an administrator, Vista wants us to confirm that we are happy with the pending action. Click Continue

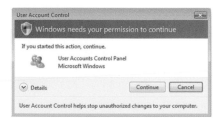

Don't forget

User Account Control even warns administrators of potentially dangerous changes. This is known as working in "Administrator Approval Mode".

5 At the Manage Accounts window, click "Create a new account"

6 At the Create New Account window, enter the name for your user, and use the default Standard user option

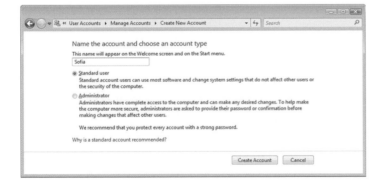

Hot tip

If your PC will have many users, it's a good idea to use a standard naming convention for your users, such as "first initial, surname". Therefore, "John Smith" would have a user name of "jsmith".

7 Click the Create Account button

Create Account

...cont'd

 Vista will return you to the Manage Accounts window. You will notice that your new user is now visible in the user list

A note about the Guest account

You may have noticed, when we set up our new account, that there was also an account in the list entitled "Guest".

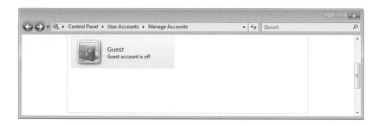

Is this an account you've created?

No. The Guest account exists for users who don't have a user profile to be able to log on to your PC.

Whilst the nature of Vista security prevents them from seeing password-protected files, folders or settings, it's best to keep the Guest account disabled, unless you have a very specific reason otherwise. Allowing the opportunity for somebody to log in to your PC without an individual profile, even under the restrictions of the Guest profile, cannot be recommended.

The Guest account is disabled under Vista by default.

Hot tip

Rather than using the Guest account, consider setting up a temporary account for anyone using your PC on a temporary basis. In this way you can control what access your temporary user will have, and remove the account again when they have finished.

Setting a password

Now that we've set up a new user profile, the most important step we need to take is to password-protect the profile. A user profile without a password is clearly a large security threat! Let's look at the two options available for setting a password.

Setting a password through Control Panel
If you, as the PC administrator, wish to allocate passwords for your users, you will need to do this via Control Panel.

1 Launch Control Panel once again, and double-click the User Accounts icon

2 Click "Manage another account"

3 Click the Continue button at the User Account Control warning

Continue

4 Click the user account, followed by "Create a password"

5 At the Create Password window, enter a password of sufficient strength, repeating in the Confirm field

Don't forget

Performing an action like this will require you to be logged on as an administrator. User Account Control will also warn you of the changes you are making.

43

Beware

Take the greatest of care if you choose to take advantage of the Password Hint option. Remember that anyone who uses the computer will be able to see the hint.

...cont'd

6 Click the Change Password button and exit out of the User Account window, and finally exit Control Panel

Setting each user's password is not always practical, and in most situations it is best to let people change passwords themselves. Educate your users on how to set their passwords interactively.

Setting a password interactively

A standard user will not be able to set or change their password through the User Accounts option in Control Panel, because this would require administrator rights.

Windows Vista allows standard users to adjust their passwords whilst logged into a session.

1 With the user signed in, hold down the Ctrl and Alt buttons simultaneously, and then press Delete. This will present a number of options

2 Click "Change a password…"

3 Leave the "Old password" field empty, and carefully type the new password identically in both the following fields

Don't forget

All passwords will need to follow the password strength policy we set in chapter 3.

4 When you're ready, click the white-arrow icon

5 Finally, click OK when Vista confirms the password change

Securing your files

Mighty volumes have been written about PC file security, and we can't hope to cover the entire scope of the topic here. However, keeping your file security clean and simple is a good strategy for keeping your data secure.

Folder and file sharing

In certain circumstances, you may feel it necessary to share your files and folders with other people, by creating "shared resources". It is vital that, should you have taken this route, you apply effective security to your shared resources.

Standard permissions

In this example, I have given Sofia access to a sub-folder within a folder I have created. I have specified that she should have "Reader" access, which means that she is able to look at the files and data within the folder, but she will be unable to make any modifications at all.

This level of access is dictated by a number of "permissions". Let's have a look at the permissions that Sofia has on the folder.

Beware

Take care when creating shared resources. These may be accessible to people over a network.

1   Navigate to the folder you want to check the permissions of: in this example a folder named "In Easy Steps"

2   Right-click the folder and click Properties

> Properties

3   At the Properties window, click the Security tab

4   Click the username you are interested in, in this case Sofia, and look at the permissions further down in the window

...cont'd

From the information on this window, you should be able to see what Sofia can do with files inside the folder. Here's what the permissions mean:

- *Full control.* The user has complete control to do anything they like with the file

- *Modify.* The user can amend the file

- *Read & execute.* The user can look at the contents of the file, and run it, if it is a program

- *List folder contents.* The user can see a list of what is inside the shared folder

- *Read.* The user can read the contents of the file

- *Write.* The user can write to the file but not delete any information

Sofia has "Read & execute", "List folder contents", and "Read" permissions to the shared folder, so she can look at the files inside the folder and open them, but she would not be able to make any changes to the information. If she were to have the "Full control" permission, she would have a free reign to do anything with the files.

Use permissions carefully to provide levels of access to files for your users. Always remember that you should allocate the minimum access level you believe to be necessary, and only increase access as necessary.

The Public folder

Though we've only scratched the very surface of Windows Vista file security, you should be able to see that sharing files and folders quickly becomes a very complex matter.

Fortunately, there is an easier way in Windows Vista of sharing your files. Vista has a folder called "Public" that is located with all the other users' folders.

The Public folder contains a number of sub-folders, including Documents, Downloads, Music, Pictures and Videos.

To share files with other users of your computer, you simply copy them into the public folders. Anyone with a username and password on your PC can access the Public folder.

Public folder security

Though the Public folder is available to anyone who has a username and password on your PC, you can apply file permissions to the files you drop into the Public folder. Therefore, you could choose to only allocate "Read" access to an important file in the Public folder, if you wanted to ensure another user couldn't make changes to it.

Public folder on the network

If your PC is part of a network, it is possible to grant access to the Public folder to people using other PCs.

- By using a feature called "password-protected sharing", you can limit network access to people who have a user account and password for your computer

- By default, network access to the Public folder is disabled. It is recommended that you leave this default setting unaltered

Hot tip

To review your sharing options, open Control Panel and double-click the Network File and Printer Sharing icon.

Using local user groups

You can allocate levels of access to user accounts on an individual basis. You can also take advantage of user "groups" to simplify administration.

Groups are collections of users that automatically inherit a pre-defined set of access levels. You can use the selection of groups that are built into Vista, or you can create your own.

The user accounts we have been using so far are already part of groups. In fact, every user account you create is automatically added to the Users group. Groups form a vital part of the Vista user account model. It is important that you are aware of how they work when dealing with user security.

Working with groups

Let's have a look at some groups in Vista.

1 Click the Start button, and then right-click Computer

2 Click the Manage option

3 Click Continue to the User Account Control message

4 A Microsoft Management Console screen will appear. Click System Tools in the left pane, and then double-click the Local Users and Groups option

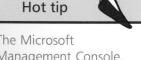

5 In the left pane, click the Groups folder. In the right pane, a list of groups will appear

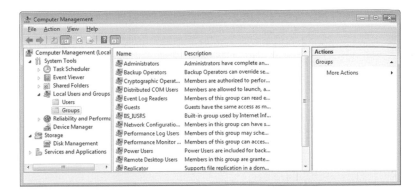

6 You may never need to use many of the groups in the list, but there are some that you need to be aware of. Firstly, double-click the Administrators group

Don't forget

Administrators can do anything on your PC! So it really does make sense to limit the use of administrator rights.

49

7 Though we have two members in this group, the Administrator account is actually disabled by default. Therefore, Mark is the only user that has administrative rights on this machine. As we have seen, it is good practice to limit administrator rights to one user account

...cont'd

8 Click Cancel, and double-click the Users group

9 Notice that the account we created earlier, Sofia, is a member of this group. The Users group gives people a level of access that prevents them from making changes that could have a damaging effect, and is thus the group that we want our standard users to be members of. When we create a standard user, they automatically gain membership of this group. Click Cancel

The Remote Desktop Users group

You should not have any members currently in the Remote Desktop Users group.

The Remote Desktop Users group requires caution. It grants specific users remote access to your PC. If you want to allow this for a specific reason temporarily, clear the group when finished.

Groups

Local user groups are useful for easing administration, but always take care when adding user accounts to the members list, and also take care when giving a group access to a file or shared resource. You need to keep in mind that you are allocating access for multiple users, and so due care is required.

Beware

The Remote Desktop feature is very handy for remote support but can also be abused by hackers for malicious purposes, if they have access to an authorized user account.

Over-the-shoulder credentials

In versions of Windows prior to Vista, a problem would occur if a standard user, without administrator rights, attempted to perform certain activities, such as:

- Changing the system time zone

- Adjusting the power management settings

- Configuring a Virtual Private Network connection

A standard user would not be able to perform these actions, as their rights would not be sufficient.

Often, administrators would add users to the local administrator group, and hence give people the rights to perform these tasks. Whilst this would seem acceptable for a responsible and trustworthy user, it introduced other implications. For instance, if the machine were to become infected with some form of malware, the malicious program would potentially have more power to make destructive changes.

The solution

The solution in Vista is "over-the-shoulder credentials". This means that users can work with standard user rights, and when they attempt to make a change to the system that requires administrator rights, the system administrator can temporarily allocate them the rights by entering their own credentials "over-the-shoulder". As the allocation of rights is temporary, it doesn't leave a lasting security gap as it would if the user were added to the local administrator group.

Hot tip

In Vista, administrators run in a mode known as "Administrator Approval Mode". This means that they are questioned by User Account Control when it detects any potentially dangerous changes being made. Whilst Administrator Approval Mode can be disabled, it is recommended that you keep it enabled, protecting your system.

Hot tip

It is recommended that over-the-shoulder credentials are used rather than adding users to the local administrator group.

Hot tip

Changes that require administrator rights will have a Windows "shield" icon.

Parental controls

The modern computing experience offers a wealth of information at the touch of a button or click of the mouse. Whilst this has transformed the options available to PC users, it has also introduced concerns. One of the most significant revolves around children using PCs, and what they may be able to access.

Modern concerns

The concerns you may have if your child uses a PC can include:

- Access to inappropriate material such as adult content

- Access to age-inappropriate games

- Interaction with anonymous users in Internet chat rooms

- Excessive periods of time spent on the PC

Parental Controls

Microsoft has developed some tools in Vista known as Parental Controls. These tools have been developed to address the concerns of parents whose children use PCs.

Beware

Whilst Internet chat rooms can provide a positive and fun environment for children, you need to be sure that they stay safe. Educate them never to give out any personal details, and if necessary limit their usage.

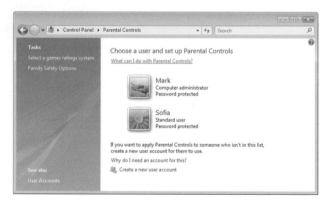

Parental Controls offer parents the ability to:

- Set time restrictions for when children can use the PC

- Control the type of game that the child can play

- Filter out inappropriate web content

- Log their child's activity in a report

- Block any other applications as necessary

Setting time limits

Let's look at setting a time limit for a child that uses a home PC.

Imagine that Chloe is regularly sneaking onto the home PC while the family are asleep in bed. Her father is concerned, and decides that allowing Chloe access to the PC from when she returns from school at 4pm, until when she goes to bed at 9pm, is a fair window of usage (although presumably he would not want her to be using the PC for the full five hours!).

1 Click the Start button, then Control Panel, and double-click the Parental Controls icon

Parental Controls

Though setting up multiple users with varying levels of security seems excessive for a home PC, parental controls show precisely why it can be a sound idea. If a child knows another username and password to use, they can easily circumvent the protection of Parental Controls.

2 Click Continue at the warning, and at the Parental Controls window select the user account you wish to apply controls to

Chloe
Standard user
Password protected

3 Adjust the Parental Controls radio button to "On, enforce current settings"

Parental Controls:
○ On, enforce current settings
○ Off

4 Click "Time limits"

Time limits
Control when Chloe uses the computer

5 In the Time Restrictions window, you will see a grid representing the full week. Simply click any hours you wish to block, and they will be marked blue. Click OK when finished, and then exit Parental Controls

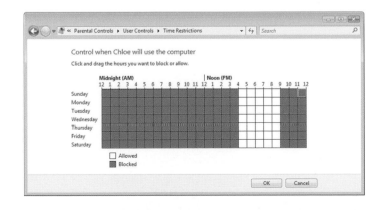

Block inappropriate content

Chloe is now unable to use the PC anywhere outside of her 4pm–9pm window, but this doesn't mean that she is safe from inappropriate material between these times.

Let's imagine that her father wants to further protect her from inappropriate material. He can take advantage of the Web Restrictions in Parental Controls.

1 Launch Parental Controls through Control Panel once again, and select the relevant user account, in our case Chloe

2 Click the Windows Vista Web Filter link

3 Ensure the "Block some websites or content" radio button is checked

4 Adjust the "Choose a web restriction level" radio button to Custom, and in the category list, tick the check boxes as appropriate

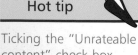

5 Click OK and OK again to return to the Parental Controls window, and close the window when done

6 The virus threat

Viruses are one of the oldest surviving computer threats, but the dangers posed by their actions have not diminished over time. Protection is still vital.

56 What is a virus?

58 Installing protection

60 Scanning your PC

61 Are you infected?

62 Preventing virus threats

63 Hoaxes

64 Viruses – think laterally

What is a virus?

Of all the threats to your PC's security, the one that has gained the most notoriety is the virus. It's no mistake that the mere mention of a computer virus can cause a PC user to shiver! Most viruses are written with malicious intent in mind, and it's important to understand how these malicious intentions have changed over the years.

Viruses – a biological comparison

Before we glance at the history of viruses, let's examine the name itself. Understanding the name "virus" helps us to understand how they work, and how to prevent them from spreading.

When we contract a virus in our body, it begins to multiply and spread throughout our system, and has the potential to spread to other people. It will almost undoubtedly have some range of unpleasant side effects. The computer virus shares almost identical attributes, in a technological sense:

- It makes copies of itself

- It attempts to spread to other systems

- It is likely that it will carry a "payload", which causes some sort of undesired effect on the victim's machine

Virus terms

As can happen in the computing world, technical terms can cause confusion and ambiguity. The term "virus" is often used as a definition to cover most malicious programs, and in terms of fighting the battle against PC threats, this can be a useful approach. However, in strict terms, we need to understand the difference between the three main threats that people tend to refer to as "viruses", as we touched upon in chapter 1:

- *Viruses*. A true virus must make copies of itself and be able to run itself too

- *Worms*. Worms use computer networks to spread, often via email systems, and can also make copies of themselves

- *Trojan horses*. A trojan horse on a PC, with similar intent to the mythical horse presented to the Trojan people, masquerades as a legitimate program but will have malicious actions when executed

56

The history of computer viruses

Many people regard "Brain" as the first true virus, because it was the first to infect the fast-rising "IBM PC", now known simply as the "PC". In its initial form, it would infect floppy disks and render the contents unreadable. Later variants of the Brain virus could also infect hard disks and cause similar data loss, which was clearly a major problem for its victims.

Methods of infection

It is valuable to understand how viruses spread. In the days of the "Brain" virus, networks were less common and the Internet was less accessible, so virus writers targeted users' reliance upon floppy disks to exchange data. Today, the world is connected via both corporate networks and the massive collection of computers on the Internet. This carves a clear route for virus writers. Many of the biggest threats to PC security come in the form of worms, which is no surprise, as worms use computer networks to spread.

Malicious intentions

Early viruses usually tried to cause some damage to the machine's operating system or data, and to show the technical prowess of the virus writer. Modern viruses (and worms, and trojan horses) are as likely to remain hidden and are often used for criminal means, whether this is to facilitate identity fraud, or to cause severe disruption in the form of direct denial of service attacks.

Virus libraries

Arm yourself with knowledge if your PC becomes infected with a virus, or if you hear of one from friends or the news. Sites such as Sophos have comprehensive libraries packed with information.

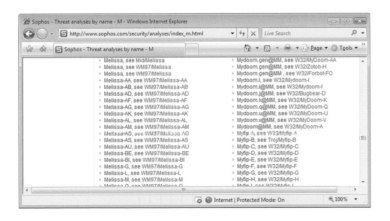

Hot tip

Viruses that are used for research or academic purposes are distinguished from viruses infecting people's PCs. "In the wild" is the term for viruses active and spreading uncontrolled across people's PCs.

Don't forget

Whilst floppy disks are used less and less now, USB flash drives and other removable media are still capable of being infected by viruses. Even CD-ROMs can arrive with viruses on board. Be careful and vigilant in checking the media you use on your PC. We'll be looking at scanning media for viruses shortly.

Hot tip

All antivirus software providers should have good-quality virus libraries or encyclopedias. Navigate to your antivirus provider's website to find it. We're looking at installing antivirus software next.

Installing protection

Now that we've gained an appreciation of what the term "virus" (and its related terms, such as "worm" and "trojan horse") can mean, and the general havoc that these nasty programs can have on our systems, we need to look at what to do to prevent ourselves from becoming victims. The first and most important step in this objective? Antivirus protection.

Installing antivirus software

Following the gloomy talk of viruses and payloads, it hopefully comes as a pleasant surprise that it is possible to gain good-quality antivirus protection for your machine for free, so long as you are a personal user. The software will protect you against viruses, including worms and trojan horses.

Avast! Antivirus

We're going to use the antivirus product Avast! to protect our PC. Avast! is a free solution for personal users.

1   Open a new session of Internet Explorer, and type in the address http://www.avast.com/eng/avast_4_home.html

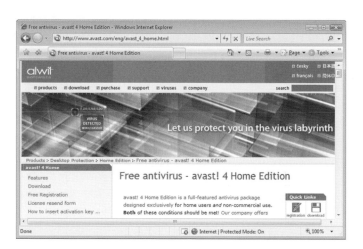

2   Click the "download" (floppy disk) icon

3   Click the Download button next to your chosen language

Hot tip

Many antivirus packages also protect you against other threats too, such as spyware. Check the details of your chosen package.

Hot tip

You will need to be logged in as an administrator to run this installation.

Hot tip

If an antivirus application is "free" for personal users, this doesn't mean that the quality will be poor. Most free options are offered to personal users by antivirus software companies that distribute their product to businesses for a fee, so the demand for a good-quality product is high.

4 At the File Download window, click Run to launch the
   setup file

5 Click Continue when the User Account
   Control window appears

6 At the Welcome window, click Next, and
   then follow the subsequent defaults, if you
   are satisfied with them, by clicking Next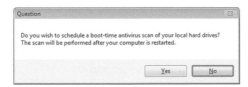
   until files begin to copy

7 When the files have finished copying, the Avast! setup
   will present a message asking if you would like a scan run
   at boot-up. Click No for the moment, because we will
   be running a manual scan ourselves next

8 At the "Setup finished" window, leave the radio button
   set to Restart

9 Make sure all of your other applications are closed, and
   click the Finish button to restart your machine

Hot tip

If you are using a dial-up
modem connection over
an analog telephone
line, you may want to
choose to save the file,
rather than to run from
the current location.
This will mean you can
re-run the saved file if
you experience problems
during setup. Using the
Run option copies the
setup file to a temporary
location and then
automatically launches.

Beware

Antivirus software
that is offered free to
"personal" users is done
so in good faith by
antivirus companies. A
"personal" user means
a home user, not
working in a business or
institution.

Scanning your PC

Now that virus protection is installed, you will notice some new icons in your system tray. Note the round icon with the letter "a".

Real time scanning

This icon is the Avast! On-Access Scanner. This part of your antivirus protection is known as "real time" protection, as it is scanning files that your PC is using as you work. The types of program files it is monitoring range from operating system files to files in your email application.

Running a complete scan

To be sure our PC is free from viruses, we need to run a full system scan over the hard drives. It is a good idea to run this regularly, to provide extra protection in addition to the On-Access Scanner.

1 Launch Avast! by selecting All Programs, "avast! Antivirus", and "avast! Antivirus" again from the Start menu

2 The Avast! interface is a car-radio-style display. We want to choose hard drives to scan, so click the Local Disks icon, and click the tick box to "Scan archive files"

3 Click the Start button to commence the scan

4 Avast! will begin scanning your computer's files and report back it's findings

Type of current scan:	Standard Scan
Tested files:	254
C:\MSOCache\All Users\90850409-6000...\WDVIEWER.CAB	
Current scanner status:	Running

Hot tip

Notice when you launch Avast!, it runs a scan over the computer's memory. This ensures that no viruses will interfere with the running of the drive scan and potentially give false results.

Hot tip

We want to scan archive files as well because viruses can hide inside these file types. The scan will take longer, as it has to extract the files to examine them, but it is a worthwhile step to take.

Hot tip

Avast! can scan removable media such as USB flash drives and CD-ROMs too. Simply run the same process as for the hard drives, but select the Removable Media button instead (you can see which one it is by hovering the mouse over it).

Are you infected?

Even with strong antivirus protection, there are still occasions when viruses are able to slip through the net and infect machines, particularly if virus definitions are not up to date.

There are a number of signs you can identify that may indicate your PC has become infected, and if you notice these you need to update your virus definitions and run a full system scan right away.

Indications of an infection

If you are experiencing unusual behavior on your PC, check it against this list. Remember that virus infections may exhibit other unusual behavior too, or they may not exhibit any noticeable behavior at all.

- Performance problems. Has your machine started to run slowly, or even freeze, requiring a reboot? Viruses run processes on your PC, and have an overhead on your machine's performance. Many viruses are poorly coded and so affect PC performance severely

- Forced reboots. The Blaster worm, as an example, caused a condition on PCs that forced Windows to reboot

- Display changes. The appearance of the system may change in some way, such as display quality, or color schemes

- Your antivirus software is closed. Some viruses attempt to close off antivirus protection so that the user is not alerted to the presence of the malicious program

- Files changed or missing. Viruses need to make adjustments to your system to do their work, so that files must be changing somewhere. They are commonly programmed to do this in stealthy fashion, but as some virus payloads involve the deletion of files, look out for anything unusual

- Application problems. Has Microsoft Word, for example, begun to behave in an unexpected way? Macro viruses utilize the power of macros to execute their malicious code. Microsoft Word will, by default, alert you to the fact that Macros are embedded in a document, but if you have the "Enable all macros" option selected in the Trust Center, it will trust all macros, even malicious ones, automatically

Don't forget

The consequences of being infected by a virus may be small in some cases, but in some other examples, they can mean that precious information such as bank details are being sent out to a remote server. If you suspect a virus infection, don't hesitate to take action.

Beware

These signs may suggest a virus infection, but they can also point to hardware or software errors on your machine. Eliminate the possibility of a virus infection first.

Beware

Macros are a useful way of automating tasks. However, because of the possibility of using programming scripts to write macros, they are able to be abused by virus writers. Take great caution with any document that has embedded macros. If in doubt, don't enable them.

Preventing virus threats

If your PC is protected with antivirus software, such as Avast! antivirus, and if you are on the lookout for the tell-tale signs of a virus infection, have you done enough to prevent a virus infection?

Not yet. Make sure you follow these golden rules to further minimize the risk of virus infection.

- Do not download anything you don't trust from the Internet

- Meticulously scan removable media, such as USB flash drives, floppy disks, and CD-ROMs

- Never run email attachments from unknown recipients. Be skeptical of email attachments even from those you know and trust, as some viruses send out infected attachments to people's entire address books

- Avoid the use of "peer to peer" file-sharing utilities, which can facilitate easy transmission of infected files

- Take care with instant messaging applications too, as these are often enhanced with file-sharing options

Updating your software's virus definitions

The final golden rule is to always keep your virus definitions up to date. New viruses are being written all of the time, and with estimates of there having been well over 70,000 viruses written throughout computing history, this is a vital requirement.

Let's run an update on the Avast! antivirus program.

1   Launch the main Avast! program, by double-clicking on the Avast! desktop icon

avast!
Antivirus

2   Click Continue to the User Account Control warning

Continue

3   At the main interface, click the lightning-bolt symbol to run the update

4   Click Close when the update is complete

Don't forget

Your virus software can only protect you against threats that it is aware of. If you don't keep your virus definitions up to date, it will have difficulty detecting new threats.

62

Hot tip

Whilst the number of viruses that have been created through PC history is a daunting one, it's a smaller percentage that actually exist in the wild at one time. So whilst virus protection is essential, it's reassuring to know that many viruses get eliminated completely.

Hoaxes

As so many people are affected by computer virus infections, some users forward on warnings about new viruses, in order to alert their friends and colleagues to a new threat.

Whilst this is a very positive activity in the interests of the PC community, it has, unfortunately, been abused. Some individuals generate "hoax" email messages and propagate them throughout email groups as quickly and as wide-spread as they can. These hoaxes usually suggest that the virus is so dangerous that an extremely severe consequence will occur, such as your hard drive being destroyed. Infamous hoaxes have included the "Budweiser screensaver" virus (which, whilst the screensaver existed, had no malicious code inside), and "A Virtual Card for You", which would allegedly wipe your hard drive.

How are hoaxes harmful?
Whilst not intrinsically harmful, hoaxes are more than a mild irritation. The effect they have upon users is to lower their vigilance, and create a tendency to reject all virus warnings as false. With PC users accustomed to receiving false virus alerts, they are less likely to respond to genuine ones.

How to deal with virus hoaxes
There are two steps you need to take with every virus alert:

1. Visit your antivirus software homepage, and check their hoax database. An example is the McAfee hoax list at http://vil.mcafee.com/hoax.asp

2. If you confirm the message to be a hoax, do not forward it any further, and tell the person who sent it to you to refrain from forwarding it too

Hot tip

Encourage people who have forwarded hoax virus alerts onto you, albeit unwittingly, to check the hoax database too. Educating yourself and others is key in the battle against viruses and hoaxes.

Don't forget

You can check up on and read about viruses and hoaxes online, using sites such as www.symantec.com, as pictured below.

Beware

It's likely that the hoaxers decided to use the jdbgmgr.exe file as the basis of their hoax because it has a distinctive "teddy bear" icon. This file looks suspect, even though it is perfectly harmless. Hoaxers use elements such as these to lead people into making rushed, ill-informed decisions.

Hot tip

The person most likely to notice the deletion of the jdbgmgr.exe file is a Java developer!

Viruses – think laterally

Virus writers are always coming up with fresh and inventive ways to cause malicious harm of various sorts, so you need to keep an open mind as to how a virus may manifest itself.

Hoax writers, whilst not nearly so technically adept, seem to equal the virus writers in the depths of their imaginations! Let's look at two important examples that teach us valuable lessons.

The Bin-Laden and Olympic Torch warning

An email was circulated recently that detailed not one but two virus warnings. The first warned of a Bin-Laden virus arriving via email that would crash your system, and the second detailed an Olympic Torch virus that would "burn" your hard drive of all data.

It may initially appear that both warnings are hoaxes, but there is a clever trick in action here. Whilst the Olympic Torch "virus" is certainly non-existent, the Bin-Laden virus did actually exist. Tying these two items together, the true and the false, lends the message more credence, especially to those who may have been aware of the Bin-Laden virus already.

The jdbgmgr.exe hoax

Victims of the jdbgmgr.exe hoax were on the receiving end of a very cunning psychological trick. Whilst the email people received was certainly a hoax, it actually managed to cause damage to many PCs, without using any code whatsoever!

The hoax worked by convincing people to delete a "virus" on their hard drive, jdbgmgr.exe. This file isn't a virus at all, but a perfectly legitimate system file! This has led some to argue that the jdbgmgr.exe hoax could actually be considered a "virus", or more strictly a "worm", as it travels across a network (via the email), issues a payload (the user deleting a file), and then moves on to infect others (the user emails their friends to do the same). With such trickery at play, you need to remain ever vigilant.

7 Security on the Internet

Ever since the explosion in popularity of the Internet, PC users have seen a whole host of new technologies enrich their computing experience. At the same time, they have also witnessed the rapid development of a bewildering range of new threats. It is especially important to protect your PC against the variety of threats that are challenging your PC's security on the world's biggest network.

66 Internet threats

67 Malware

68 Vista Internet security

69 Spyware – educate yourself

70 Windows Defender

73 Anti-spyware alternatives

74 Internet browsing tips

75 Online banking services

77 Clearing your history

78 Internet certificates

79 Rogue dialers

80 IE security settings

85 IE advanced settings

86 Using the pop-up blocker

88 Turning off auto-complete

89 Disabling add-ons

90 Windows Firewall

95 Testing your security level

Internet threats

As we saw in chapter 1, today's PCs have the widest range of threats to defend against. This situation has evolved due to the dynamics of the modern PC. Your PC is likely to be attached to a network of some description, including the world's largest computer network, the Internet, which can bring threats in the form of:

- Viruses
- Spyware and adware
- Other malware, such as rootkits, keystroke loggers, and rogue dialers
- Hackers and other online criminals
- Other threats to your PC's security

Internet connection implications

The dynamics of the PC have changed in other ways too. In years gone by, the main method of choice for connecting to the Internet was the analog phone-line dial-up over a 56k (or lower) modem. Whilst the performance didn't match that of today's vastly superior broadband connections, in security terms it had some clear benefits:

- Users would dial up, surf, and disconnect again. The window of opportunity for hackers, viruses and other threats to make their way onto the PC was therefore far smaller
- The slower connection speed meant that the threats had less bandwidth with which to complete their malicious tasks

Many people have "always-on" broadband connections today, which means we have to be extra vigilant when securing our PCs.

Connecting an unsecured PC to the Internet

Whilst I can't recommend that you try it, it is certainly an interesting experience to connect a PC to the Internet without any security protection at all.

Whilst a few years ago you could surf for a considerable period of time before threats began to emerge, an unsecured PC today will only last for a limited time on the Internet before viruses, pop-ups and other threats attach themselves to the machine.

Don't forget

When your PC is under threat, so is the data stored on your PC.

Hot tip

Dial-up users using analog phone lines still need to take the greatest of care on the Internet, and the measures in this book will be helping people still using this connection method.

Beware

You are at a heightened level of vulnerability while using online banking services, and we will be looking at how to protect our valuable data at these times.

Malware

We covered the various threats facing your PC in chapter 1, but for the purposes of this chapter, it's a worthwhile exercise to have a brief re-cap of the main threats that target your PC while you are attached to the Internet.

Viruses

Viruses, worms and trojan horses can be contracted over the Internet, whether passed from web pages to your local machine, or traveling between "peer-to-peer" file-sharing programs.

Spyware

Spyware is a prolific threat to your PC while attached to the Internet. Whilst it usually requires user intervention for installation, it often achieves this through deceptive means, whether this is masquerading as legitimate software, or installing itself during another application's installation routine. It aims to collect and transmit your personal information to a third party, whether this is advertisers or criminals.

Adware

Adware is also a prolific threat to your PC. It aims to install itself in similar fashion to spyware, and then bombards you with advertising, which may be specifically targeted according to your browsing habits. This data may have been gleaned from spyware!

Zombie PC

If your PC becomes infected by some types of malware, it can potentially be transformed into a zombic PC by a hacker. This means that the remote user can abuse your PC as they choose.

DDoS attacks

If your PC's security is compromised by a hacker and becomes a zombie PC, it can be used for a "direct denial of service" attack. This means it is part of a group of PCs that are being abused for the purpose of bringing down a server or website.

Keystroke loggers

Keystroke loggers capture every keystroke you make. This will include usernames, passwords, and any sensitive data you type. They can infect your machine via viruses and worms.

Phishing websites

Phishers set up fake websites to attempt to gain personal details.

Beware

Peer-to-peer file-sharing programs can be havens for viruses, and may also introduce copyright issues. In this light they are best avoided.

Beware

Ironically, spyware often masquerades as security software to persuade people to install it!

Beware

If you are using a dial-up connection over an analog phone line, you also need to be aware of rogue dialers, which attempt to make a connection to a premium-rate phone line. We will be looking at protecting against the threats dialers pose too.

Vista Internet security

As we've seen, Windows Vista has been built from the ground up with a firm focus on providing a secure computing environment for users. We've also seen how modern users have the widest ever range of threats facing them due to the interconnected nature of the modern PC.

Windows Vista

New security features in Windows Vista include:

- *Windows Defender.* Windows Defender is a real advantage for modern PC users in the fight against spyware, adware, and other types of malware. It not only scans your PC for these threats, but also protects in "real time", meaning that threats are detected at the earliest possible opportunity, rather than being uncovered in a later scan

- *Windows Firewall.* Windows Firewall, the integral software firewall, has been updated and improved to provide even stronger protection for your machine against online threats

Internet Explorer 7

Internet Explorer, with the release of version 7, has also seen some major security improvements:

- New coding resulting in even stronger online security

- Phishing website detection. Internet Explorer 7 includes a new phishing filter which compares sites visited against a list of known phishing sites, and can send details of suspicious sites back to Microsoft for further investigation. It also looks for common characteristics of phishing websites and presents a warning if it finds anything suspicious

- Internet Protection Mode. Working in this mode places barriers to help prevent various types of malware from installing on your PC

Spyware – educate yourself

Many providers of antispyware programs help you to educate yourself against the threats out there, such as on the AdAware antimalware package website at www.lavasoft.com.

Educating yourself about specific threats

Other websites provide information about specific malware threats, such as the www.spywareguide.com website:

Is it a genuine download?

Whilst there isn't a de facto standard in place, there are some agencies that provide verification of genuine downloads. Since many spyware packages actually disguise themselves as antispyware tools, it's reassuring to see a familiar icon when downloading a file, that vouches for its safety.

69

Hot tip

If you want to check that a verification of authenticity by a third party is valid, click the link to visit the website and view the information. In the example on the left, Softpedia is verifying that a download is genuine, and you can click the image to visit their website.

Windows Defender

In response to the rapidly growing threat posed by spyware, and as part of the drive to create a robust and secure operating system, Microsoft has developed an antispyware solution that comes as an integral part of the Windows Vista operating system.

The aptly named Windows Defender has three methods of helping protect your machine from the prying eyes of spyware.

Real time defense

Windows Defender runs in real time. This means that it is constantly monitoring what is trying to run on your PC, and it will alert you when any potentially malicious programs try to install themselves.

Scans

Defender runs traditional scans too. This can be compared to running an antivirus scan on your computer, but searching for spyware as opposed to viruses. By default, Defender will schedule a daily scan at 02:00. It is recommended that you keep this default in place, for maximum protection against any malicious programs that may have slipped past the real time protection.

Microsoft SpyNet

Online communities can be an excellent way of sharing knowledge for the mutual benefit of all concerned. The SpyNet community provides information on what other users have allowed to run on their PCs, and builds community ratings to help you make accurate judgements and choices.

Microsoft SpyNet
Join the online community that helps identify and stop spyware infections

Definitions

Just as with antivirus software, antispyware software is only as good as your latest definitions file. Windows Defender is tightly integrated with the Windows Update feature, and together they work towards ensuring that Defender is prepared to deal with the latest threats that may harm your PC.

Hot tip

Antispyware packages can also help you against other malware threats such as dialers, rootkits, trojan horses, worms, keystroke loggers, remote access tools, and bot software. Check the documentation of your chosen package.

Don't forget

Many defaults in Windows Vista are set to give you maximum security benefit and are best left in place.

Hot tip

By default, Windows Defender is set to update your definitions file before the daily scan. This is a clear example of carefully selected defaults in Windows Vista.

Let's explore the Windows Defender interface and look at some key areas that you will need to be aware of. Whilst the defaults are a good base to work from, it is worth knowing which options are available to you so that you can tailor them to your own preferences.

 To access Windows Defender settings, click the Start button, followed by Control Panel

 Next, double-click the Windows Defender icon, and the main interface appears

Windows Defender

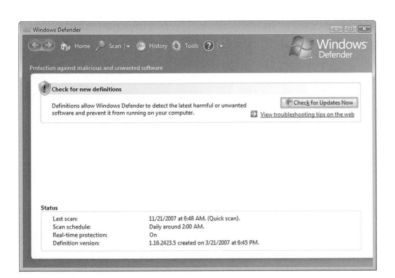

 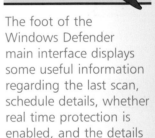
If Windows Defender displays a green shield, you can rest assured that the definitions are up to date and there are no discovered spyware threats. If there is a problem, such as out-of-date definitions, Defender will notify you, as in the example above

If you wish to run a scan immediately, click the Scan button

Click the Tools button to see some further options

6 The Tools window presents further options. If you wish to make tweaks to the way Defender runs, click Options in the Settings group. It's best to keep the default settings to maintain tight security, unless you have specific requirements

7 Use the Microsoft SpyNet button to join the SpyNet community and share information about spyware

8 The Software Explorer option is a useful glance at the programs running on your PC, allowing you to identify any spyware that has bypassed your security

9 Use the "Quarantined items" button to manage software that Windows has stopped from running on your PC. Take care if choosing to restore this software

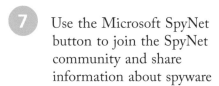

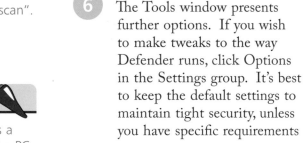

Antispyware alternatives

Windows Defender provides a high level of protection for your PC against spyware and adware. There are alternative antispyware packages available, and you can try these out as well.

Some PC users regularly use different antispyware packages. This can be a useful approach, as different packages can detect different threats. Using another antispyware program from time to time can minimize the risk of infection. This is not a shortcoming of any particular antispyware choice. It is almost impossible for any package to be aware of every spyware or malware threat in existence!

AdAware

One of the earliest antispyware packages with a huge user base across the world, Lavasoft's AdAware is a solid contender for your antispyware package of choice. Try it out at www.lavasoft.com.

The "SE Personal" edition of AdAware is free for personal use, but doesn't include real time scanning. You can upgrade to have this option by purchasing the "SE Plus" edition.

Spybot Search & Destroy

Spybot Search & Destroy is another solid antispyware choice. Whilst there is currently no full real time option, it is well worth running a Spybot Search & Destroy scan over your PC from time to time as a safety net to catch any missed threats.

Don't forget

Windows Defender provides a high level of protection by monitoring your PC for threats in "real time", as well as offering the option to scan at scheduled times, or whenever you please. If you opt for a different package, consider if it is going to offer you the same level of protection.

Beware

Trying out different antispyware packages is a sound idea, but beware of tools claiming to have found threats on your machine before you've even downloaded them. Many spyware items try to "trick" users by masquerading as antispyware packages!

Beware

It's possible that you may have unknowingly authorized some spyware being installed on your machine, by accepting another application's license agreement that installs the spyware at the same time. Always check the license agreement you are accepting!

Internet browsing tips

Hot tip

Why not incorporate these guidelines into your security document, and explain the details to the other users of your PC?

Beware

Identity fraud is on the increase, so you must take every caution when entering your bank details and other personal information online.

Beware

A cunning trick played by some malicious sources involves using double extensions in a filename, for instance freegame.txt.exe. If you download the file and have the "Hide extensions for known file types" option enabled in Windows Explorer File Options, you may think the file is a plain-text file. It will actually run the file as an executable file when launched, which could pose a threat to your PC.

In chapter 3, we explored the reasons why users can often unwittingly pose one of the biggest threats to your PC's security.

Using the Internet is an activity where the chances of a PC user introducing dangers to your PC hits something of a peak! While online, users are susceptible to spyware infections, adware infections, worms, trojan horses, phishing attempts, social-engineering attempts, and hacking efforts, amongst other threats. Let's look at some Internet browsing tips to stay safe online:

- Avoid clicking links to websites that are offering huge rewards and clearly unrealistic offers. If it looks too good to be true, it probably is

- Don't download and use peer-to-peer file-sharing applications, sometimes referred to as "P2P" programs. These packages can increase the chances of downloading dangerous files, open your machine up to hackers and malicious programs, and can often implicate you in illegal sharing activity

- Avoid websites with dubious content

- When purchasing online or using online banking services, check the security report before you enter any personal data, including passwords. Click the padlock symbol at the right of the address bar for details, and click View Certificate to check the certificate of the site. We'll be looking more closely at online banking and certificates later in the chapter

- Exercise due caution when downloading files. Be especially careful to ensure you trust the website concerned when downloading files that end in .exe, .bat, .zip, .bas, .cmd, .com, .js, .jse, .lnk, .msi, .pif, .reg, .scr, .vb, .vbe, .vbs, .wsc and .wsf. All of these file types can be used by malicious sources, so be careful, and if in doubt, don't download or run these files

- Be extremely careful if you use Internet chat rooms and forums. Never give out any personal information, even if it seems innocuous. It is particularly important to pass this advice on to children, who often aren't aware of the dangers

Online banking services

It's no exaggeration to say that the Internet and the World Wide Web have transformed our lives and how we perform certain tasks. One of the biggest benefits of this transformation is the ability to perform banking transactions and maintenance from the comfort of your own home.

It should come as no surprise that online banking is the leading target for online criminals, and this is where you must tread most carefully while working online. Let's run through the steps required for the ideal secure online banking experience.

1 Open Internet Explorer and visit your online banking site by manually typing in the address or following a favorite that you have made. Never follow a link from an email, as it may be from a phisher, even if it looks authentic

2 Ensure nobody is looking over your shoulder while you log in, and check the certificate of the site using the padlock icon, as mentioned in "Internet browsing tips"

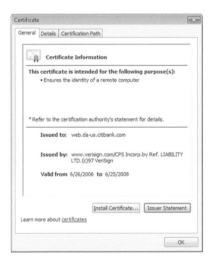

3 The longer you spend online, the more opportunity online threats, such as hackers or automated programs, will have to compromise your security. Therefore, it's a good idea to think of what you want to do before logging in to the website, and then completing your transactions carefully and swiftly while you are logged in

Beware

Whilst some are still particularly crude, online criminals are, on the whole, becoming better at copying the "look and feel" of genuine websites, and may have "lifted" graphics and other elements from the genuine website. Exercise particular caution when using banking services online.

Hot tip

While using online banking, you will need to be protected by a firewall. We'll be looking at Windows Firewall later in this chapter, and then a hardware firewall in chapter 9.

Hot tip

Do not write down, share, or save to a file your online banking access information. Keep it very safe.

...cont'd

Hot tip

We'll be looking more closely at the email side of phishing in chapter 8, "Email security".

Hot tip

Phishers' email address databases are often harvested using illegitimate means such as spyware, and programs that trawl web pages to capture addresses. This reinforces the importance of securing your PC from spyware and taking care with posting your email address.

Beware

If a phisher successfully extracts banking details from a victim, they will attempt to use the details for purchases, to sell on to other criminals, or to perform other forms of identity fraud. If you have any concerns about an online banking experience, contact your bank straightaway.

④ Ensure that you log out of your online banking website as soon as you have finished using the service, and then close the window entirely. Many online banking services automatically log you out after a set period of inactivity

The Vista anti-phishing filter

Online phishing attempts are often working in tandem with phishing emails. The process a phisher follows when trying to steal banking details follows a general pattern:

● The phisher sends out a raft of speculative emails to a huge email address database

● Many recipients will delete or ignore the email as they don't bank with the institution the phisher is masquerading as

● Of the recipients who do bank with the selected institution, many will recognize the email as false and delete or ignore the email, or it will be filtered by their security software

● If the phisher is successful, some individuals will accept the message as genuine and follow the false link to the online banking website. This will be the phisher's own web server, designed to capture the user's bank account details

Whilst there is no substitute for vigilance and caution, Vista's anti-phishing filter can help to prevent the success of phishing attempts on your PC. When you first use Internet Explorer after Vista has been installed, you are prompted to enable the anti-phishing filter. Accept the default radio-button choice of "Turn on automatic Phishing Filter (recommended)" and click OK.

> ● **Turn on automatic Phishing Filter (recommended)**
> Some website addresses will be sent to Microsoft to be checked. Information received will not be used to personally identify you.
>
> ● **Turn off automatic Phishing Filter**
> Website addresses will not be sent to Microsoft unless you choose to check them.
>
> ○ Ask me later

If you have missed this prompt or taken the wrong option, you can open Internet Explorer and press Alt, click the Tools menu option, select Internet Options…, click the Advanced tab, and in the Phishing Filter group click the "Turn on automatic website checking" radio button.

Clearing your history

Returning to our comparison of PC security with the security of your home, what would be the extra benefit to a burglar if you left her some inadvertent "clues" in the form of documents, letters, and other important items?

The benefit to the intruder would probably be considerable. Leaving your web browsing history uncleared could grant the same benefit to any "virtual" intruders to your PC. If they managed to log onto your PC with your user account (just as the burglar "breaks" into your home), and saw that you had visited, for instance, the Barclays Bank Internet banking website, then they would have a headstart on breaking into your account.

With this example in mind, it's good practice to regularly clear Internet Explorer's history of websites you have visited, and also the temporary Internet files that are stored on your computer.

Hot tip

You may hear people refer to clearing temporary Internet files as "clearing the cache".

Hot tip

Internet Explorer holds a "cache" of pages, images, and other files that are transferred to your computer when you visit a web page. This is to enable faster browsing when you return to a previously visited website, as much of the information, if unchanged, can be accessed directly from your cache of files. With today's high-speed connections, the benefits aren't so noticeable, and security considerations should come first.

1 Open Internet Explorer, and click the Tools button at the top right of the window

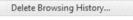

2 Click on the Delete Browsing History… option

3 Whilst you could choose to delete the various areas of browsing history individually, it's safest to remove all browsing history by clicking "Delete all…"

4 Click Yes to confirm the removal of browsing history. You may want to leave the "Also delete files and settings stored by add-ons" check box unticked if you make special use of certain add-ons

Internet certificates

When you want to purchase a product or service over the Internet, or if you want to log in to your bank's online services, how can you be sure that the website you are visiting is the site it purports to be? How can you tell that your data can't be intercepted by others?

This is where digital certificates can help. A certificate contains verification from a trusted, independent authority, known as a certification authority, that the website is indeed the site it claims to be. It also offers encryption, or "scrambling" during the exchange of data, using SSL (Secure Socket Layer) or TLS (Transport Layer Security) technology, so that you can be sure your information is not being revealed to prying eyes.

Let's take a look at digital certificates in action.

 Beware

The fact that a website presents the padlock icon in the address bar doesn't mean that it is a legitimate site. Always check the certificate details to be certain.

Hot tip

Large certification authorities include VeriSign, Comodo, Entrust, and Go Daddy.

Hot tip

Internet Explorer will display a warning if the certificate has expired, or if there is another issue with the certificate. Should this happen, do not use the website to transmit any personal details whatsoever.

1 Launch Internet Explorer, and visit a site that requires security of transmitted data, such as an online store or an online banking service. In this example we're going to visit the Citibank.com website

2 When the page has loaded, click the "Sign on" link

Sign on

3 Notice the padlock icon in the far right of the address bar. Click the padlock, and you will see that the certification authority VeriSign has identified the site and has a certificate available for viewing

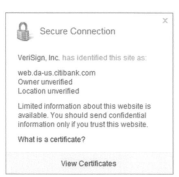

Secure Connection

VeriSign, Inc. has identified this site as:

web.da-us.citibank.com
Owner unverified
Location unverified

Limited information about this website is available. You should send confidential information only if you trust this website.

What is a certificate?

View Certificates

4 Click View Certificates, and you'll notice that VeriSign has provided independent verification that the identity of the site we are using is accurate

Issued to: web.da-us.citibank.com

Issued by: www.verisign.com/CPS Incorp.by Ref. LIABILITY LTD.(c)97 VeriSign

Valid from 6/26/2006 to 6/25/2008

78

Rogue dialers

If you've ever known anyone who has been the unfortunate victim of a rogue dialer, or even worse, you have been the victim of a rogue dialer yourself, you'll be keen to do whatever you can to avoid allowing this type of malicious software onto your PC.

What is a dialer?

Whilst dialers have legitimate purposes, such as for facilitating a modem connection to your Internet service provider, rogue dialers abuse the nature of the program by tricking users into clicking a button to dial a specific telephone number, usually at a premium rate. They may also install themselves without your knowledge, or install themselves whether you click "yes" to install or "no" to decline install.

Let's look at some measures you can take.

Use a broadband connection

Rogue dialers are a product of the age when the modem dial-up connection reigned supreme as the dominant mode of Internet access. Broadband connections are usually immune to this form of malware, so if you are still looking for a reason to make the upgrade to the faster connection, and your area offers the broadband service, it's worth adding this justification to the list.

Keep antispyware software up to date

Just as we need to keep our antivirus definitions up to date, it is essential that spyware definitions stay up to date too. Whilst rogue dialers are less prevalent than before, there is no guarantee that new ones won't be released to target PCs like yours.

Common sense

Perhaps the most powerful tool in your security toolbox is, as with much PC security, common sense. Stay away from dubious offers of "free" adult content, look out for Windows warning you of unexpected software installs, ensure your modem is unplugged or switched off at all times when offline, and listen out for it dialling when you haven't asked it to.

Removal

If you have been infected and your antispyware software won't remove the dialer, search your chosen antispyware site for manual removal details, and follow these carefully.

Beware

Rogue dialers usually use adult content as a lure to snare their victims.

Beware

Sometimes the first people know of being infected by a rogue dialer is when they receive a shock in the form of an inflated phone bill. The cumulative costs of the premium calls can end up being considerable, and the chances are that you won't be able to retrieve any of the money you've involuntarily spent.

Hot tip

Teenagers are often blamed as a result of the mischief caused by rogue dialers! If you receive a phone bill with a bulk of premium-rate calls, check your PC for the presence of this type of malware first.

IE security settings

We've learned that while using the Internet, your PC is vulnerable to a wide range of security threats from a vast array of sources. As a consequence, Internet Explorer offers a range of security settings that you can customize, and by using "zones" you can gain full flexibility of security across different network types.

Let's explore the security settings in more detail.

 Open Internet Explorer, and click Tools in the top right of the window

 Select Internet Options…   Internet Options

Click the Security tab, and have a look at the options on offer

Zones are of central importance to understanding the options before you. The "Internet" zone is currently highlighted, and any change we make while this zone is selected will affect this zone only

Notice that the Enable Protected Mode check box is ticked for this zone. It is recommended that you leave Protected Mode enabled, as it helps to prevent malicious software from the Internet gaining access to your PC

6 You can manually adjust the settings for any zone by clicking the "Custom level…" button

7 As a rule, the more options you have disabled for a zone, the safer browsing that zone will be. Of course, more options disabled means more functionality disabled, so disabling a raft of options may prove impractical and adversely affect your browsing experience. If you are not sure about one of the settings for a zone, set it to "prompt" so that you can at least tell when that setting is taking effect and then judge whether you want to allow the action accordingly

The "Local intranet" zone

The "Local intranet" zone operates according to its security settings when visiting any website that resides upon your corporate network. As many businesses now have intranet sites for employees, and applications accessible through standard browsers such as Internet Explorer, the "Local intranet" zone is a useful zone to be able to configure separately.

1 In the Security tab of Internet Options, click the "Local intranet" zone icon

2 Notice that the default level for this zone is "Medium-low". Your corporate or home network should be safer than the Internet, with fewer security threats and hacking attempts. Also, it's likely that browser-based applications may require lower levels of security in order to allow certain controls or scripts to run

The "Trusted sites" zone

If you have a website (or websites) that requires certain security options to be disabled, don't disable these settings in the "Internet" zone, as you will compromise your PC's security. A far better option is the "Trusted sites" zone, where you can allow sites specified by you to have a set level of security.

Let's have a look at how we add a website to the "Trusted sites" zone.

Let's imagine that your online banking website isn't working for you, and the technical support department there has told you that you need to make some adjustments to your browser security. Now, you immediately realize that you don't want to adjust your "Internet" zone settings, so you decide that the best course of action is to add the bank's online banking address to your "Trusted sites" zone.

 Click the "Trusted sites" icon. Notice that the security level is set to "Medium" by default, and because this will constitute a list of sites we trust, Protected Mode is not enabled for this zone

Click the Sites button

In the "Add this website to the zone" field, enter the address of the online banking website, and click the Add button. The address will appear in the Websites list, and Internet Explorer will use your "Trusted sites" zone settings for this and any other sites you add to the list

Hot tip

The "Trusted sites" zone can be useful when investigating why some websites don't seem to be working for you. For instance, some banking websites require certain security options to be disabled, and if you trust the website you could add it to the "Trusted sites" list and adjust your settings as necessary.

82

Click Close to return to the Internet Options Security tab

The "https" prefix

You may have noticed that you can only add websites to the "Trusted sites" list if the web address begins with "https". Web sites at "https" addresses ensure that the data you exchange with the site is encrypted and hence protected from prying eyes. It is recommended that you don't untick the option enabling this.

The "Restricted sites" zone

Let's imagine that you want to gain some information from a website, but are unsure whether it is safe or not. Or perhaps another user of your PC is visiting a site that you don't wish to ban, but you would like to ensure that it cannot do any damage to your system.

This is where the "Restricted sites" zone comes into play. Any websites placed into the "Restricted sites" zone are treated with most security settings set to "disabled", to prevent dangerous actions being carried out. So, ActiveX controls, for example, are disabled and cannot run. Consider placing any website that you are unsure about into this category.

1 Having accessed the Internet Options window in Internet Explorer by clicking Tools and Internet Options..., click the Security tab. Highlight the "Restricted sites" zone

2 Click the Sites button

3 In the "Restricted sites" window, enter the name of the website you would like to reside in the "Restricted sites" zone and click Add

Hot tip

Websites communicating over an address beginning with "https" use either TLS or SSL to encrypt your data, and they use digital certificates signed by certification authorities, as we explored earlier in the chapter.

...cont'd

Hot tip

The default security level of the "Restricted sites" zone is set to "High". For the safety of your machine, you cannot adjust this default.

Beware

Whilst the "Restricted sites" zone is handy, consider carefully whether you need to visit a potentially dangerous website at all. If you have instinctive concerns about a certain website, it is probably best left unvisited.

Hot tip

While working with zones in the Security tab of the Internet Options window, you can set an individual zone back to default settings by highlighting the specific zone and clicking "Default level". To reset all of the zones to defaults, click the "Reset all zones to default level" button.

4 Click Close, and then OK to return to Internet Explorer

Resetting a zone back to the default level

If you've been making extensive adjustments to your zone settings, you may want to set them back to defaults and start again. This could be a realistic prospect if you are concerned that your changes may have lowered security, or if they have introduced unexpected results in your web browsing experience

Let's see how we reset a zone back to the default level.

1 Open Internet Explorer, click Tools, Internet Options…, and then select the Security tab

2 Click the icon for the zone you wish to reset

3 Click the "Default level" button   Default level

Resetting all zones back to the default level

You may wish to set all zones back to the default level.

1 While still in the Security tab, click the "Reset all zones to default level" button   Reset all zones to default level

2 Click OK to return to Internet Explorer

IE advanced settings

Internet Explorer contains a number of advanced settings so that you can customize how your browser operates.

The defaults have been chosen with security in mind, and are hence a good selection to use. There is perhaps one option that you may wish to change. Let's have a look.

1 Open an Internet Explorer window, and click Tools, then Internet Options…, to access the Internet Options window

2 Click the Advanced tab

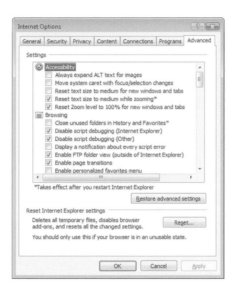

3 There are a lot of advanced options! We want to change the option "Warn if changing between secure and not secure mode". Scroll down to this option and place a tick in the check box to its left

☑ Warn if changing between secure and not secure mode

4 Ticking this box means that Internet Explorer will prompt us when we are leaving a secure site and moving to a non-secure one. Never enter any personal information into a non-secure site. Click OK to return to the Internet Explorer browser window

Hot tip

Whilst the advanced options have been designed with security in mind, you can uncheck some of the options if you want even more security. Remember that there is always a trade-off between security and functionality.

Hot tip

If you make too many changes to the Advanced tab options and are worried it could compromise the security of your PC, you can click the "Restore advanced settings" button to return to the safety of the default values.

Hot tip

It's useful to know when you are moving from a secure site to a non-secure site. You need to know when you can transmit data securely, and when the data you enter may be vulnerable. "Warn if changing between secure and not secure mode" keeps us alert to such changes.

Using the pop-up blocker

Most PC security threats arise from the abuse of perfectly legitimate features or applications. Pop-up windows are an excellent example. At one time in Internet history, pop-up windows, often known simply as "pop-ups", were used as legitimate tools for navigating through a website. Where they appeared with advertisements, this was often limited to a single window which could be easily closed, and this was seen as reasonable practice since many websites relied upon advertising revenue to survive.

However, nowadays pop-ups can be simply annoying, or they can present a very genuine security threat. As a result, Internet Explorer contains a pop-up blocker to help keep this particular threat to a minimum. Let's have a look at how we can use the pop-up blocker.

1 Open up an Internet Explorer session, and click Tools, followed by Internet Options…

2 Select the Privacy tab

3 The pop-up blocker is enabled by default, with the tick placed in the check box. It is strongly recommended that you keep this option enabled

4 Click the Settings button in the right of the Pop-up Blocker section

5 Notice the "Filter level" section at the foot of the window. If you never want any pop-ups, you can adjust this to "High: Block all pop-ups". Remember that this will also block legitimate pop-ups too, so you may want to stay with the "Medium: Block most automatic pop-ups" level

Adding exceptions

It is likely that there are certain sites you trust, and if these employ pop-ups you can add them to an exception list, so that all pop-ups from that site are allowed.

1 In Internet Explorer, click Tools, Internet Options..., select the Privacy tab, and click the Settings button

2 In the field below "Address of website to allow", type the full address of the site you wish to trust for pop-ups, and click Add

3 The website address will appear in the "Allowed sites" list

4 Click Close, and then OK to close Internet Options

Don't forget

Most PC security involves some sort of trade-off, and the pop-up blocker is no exception. Whilst blocking all pop-ups will increase your security rating, it may also prevent you from accessing content you would otherwise have benefitted from.

Hot tip

When the pop-up blocker blocks a pop-up, it will notify you at the top of the web page in an area called the "Information Bar", with a message stating "Pop-up blocked". If you want to see pop-ups from this site for this session, click the bar and select Temporarily Allow Pop-ups. If you wish to add the site to the "Allowed sites" list, select "Always Allow Pop-ups from This Site...", and click Yes to confirm.

Turning off auto-complete

The Internet Explorer auto-complete function is a handy feature that can "remember" web addresses, data you have entered into forms, and user names and passwords entered into forms.

Whilst useful and time-saving, this is not always a desirable situation. Should an unauthorized user gain access to your PC, and log in with your details, they would be able to see the websites you have visited, and be able to use stored usernames and passwords. Therefore, it is recommended that you don't allow Internet Explorer to remember any of these elements.

1 Open an Internet Explorer session, click the Tools button, select Internet Options…, and click the Content tab

2 In the AutoComplete section of the window, click the Settings button

3 Remove the ticks from any of the first three check boxes according to your security needs

4 Click OK, and then OK again to finish

Hot tip

If websites feature their own methods of remembering your username and password, usually in a "cookie", it is advisable to untick any check boxes that give you such options.

Beware

Though auto-completing web addresses may seem innocuous enough, it could give an unauthorized user "clues" as to where you have visited. Would you want them to have a headstart by discovering the address of your online banking site?

Beware

Even after disabling the auto-complete function, Internet Explorer will still have remembered any information entered up until that point. Run through the "Clearing your history" section from earlier in this chapter once again to remove this vulnerability.

Disabling add-ons

Internet Explorer supports the use of add-ons. Add-ons are small programs that work within Internet Explorer to provide extra functionality and enhancements.

A popular example of an add-on is Adobe Flash. Add-ons such as Flash can add some very useful and exciting features and functionality to your web browsing experience.

However, some add-ons can be exploited to compromise the security of your system, and some add-ons are specifically designed, by malicious elements, to provide backdoors and vulnerabilities for hackers and rogue software to abuse.

If you feel an add-on could be compromising the security of your PC, or you believe that the add-on itself is designed with malicious intentions, you should disable it immediately.

1 Open an Internet Explorer session, click the Tools button, select Internet Options…, and click the Programs tab

2 In the "Manage add-ons" section, click the "Manage add-ons" button

3 Highlight the add-on you wish to disable, and in the Settings area, adjust the radio button to Disable

4 Click OK, OK, and OK again, and restart Internet Explorer for the setting to take effect

Hot tip

Add-ons are sometimes referred to as plug-ins, snap-ins, or extensions. Add-ons are available for other applications too.

Don't forget

No enhancement that substantially compromises the security of your system is worth using.

Hot tip

You may notice an add-on in your list entitled "Research", which has no publisher name. You don't need to disable this add-on. It is installed when you install the Microsoft Office 2003 software suite.

Windows Firewall

In terms of building and construction, a firewall is a part of a building that provides protection against the threat of fire. Where one part of a building may catch fire, the firewall prevents it from spreading to the part of the building on the other side of the wall.

With the advent of networking and the rise of the world's largest network, the Internet, the concept of a firewall has become an essential element of modern computing. A firewall protects your PC from external threats by using a security policy to control the network information that travels between your computer and networks, including the Internet. Windows Vista contains an integrated firewall "out of the box" to protect you while online.

Make sure it is enabled
Let's see how we can ensure that Windows Firewall is active.

1. Click the Windows Start button, followed by Control Panel

2. Double-click the Windows Firewall icon

3. Click "Change settings"

4. Click Continue at the User Account Control warning, and at the Windows Firewall window, ensure the window reports that Windows Firewall is on

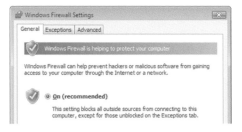

5. If, for any reason, the Windows Firewall is off, click Change Settings, then Continue, and adjust the radio button to "On (recommended)", closing the windows when you have finished

If you are a notebook user, you may connect to the Internet over a wireless connection in public places such as hotels or airports. If so, you may wish to block all incoming connections from accessing your computer over the network, on a temporary basis.

Blocking all programs

Windows Firewall offers an easy way of blocking all programs from accessing your machine.

1. Click Start, and then Control Panel, double-click the Windows Firewall icon, click the "Turn Windows Firewall on or off" link, and press Continue when the User Account Control warning message appears

2. At the Windows Firewall screen, click the "Block all incoming connections" check box

Don't forget

If you choose to block all incoming connections while working on a public network, remember to remove the tick from the "Block all incoming connections" check box when you return to your secure local network!

Hot tip

If an unauthorized program attempts to access your computer over the Internet, Windows Firewall will warn you and ask if you want to grant access. If you don't know what it is that is requesting access, then don't allow it.

3. Click OK, and then close Windows Firewall and Control Panel. Windows Firewall is now blocking any programs that attempt to access your PC over the network connection, and it is recommended that you keep this setting enabled every time you use public-access connections

...cont'd

Blocking all incoming connections makes for a very secure PC, and is ideal for when you are attached to a public network, but it restricts any legitimate programs that you may wish to allow to transfer information to and from the Internet.

The premise that Windows Firewall is based upon is that security is strongest when everything is blocked, and then only selected programs are allowed through the "doors" of the firewall. This is significantly stronger than allowing all programs access and only blocking the ones that you think could cause a threat.

Using Windows Firewall exceptions

Windows Firewall exceptions are the programs that have been explicitly granted access through the security of the firewall.

It's quite possible that you may wish to manipulate the list of exceptions. You may consider a program that is currently blocked as safe to have access to your PC, and need to add it to the exceptions list. You may also consider another program to be a threat to your PC's security, and wish to remove it from the exceptions list. Let's see how we can do this by imagining that another user has enabled File and Printer Sharing as an exception.

1 Access the Windows Firewall settings by clicking Start, Control Panel, double-clicking the Windows Firewall icon, clicking the Change Settings link, and pressing Continue to the User Account Control warning message

2 Click the Exceptions tab

3 Remove the tick from the File and Printer Sharing check box

4 Click OK, and then close the other windows we've opened

Beware

It's no coincidence that we've chosen File and Printer Sharing as an exception that we want to remove. While enabled it presents a clear risk to your PC's security and could, if not set up securely, compromise the security of the files on your PC. Windows Vista has this exception unchecked by default for these security reasons.

Hot tip

You can manually add program exceptions if they don't appear in the list. From the Windows Firewall exceptions tab, click "Add program...", and either select a program from the list, or manually browse to the program file using the Browse... button.

We've learned how to work with exceptions in Windows Firewall, which means we can choose which programs can and can't use our computer over the Internet.

Windows Firewall also blocks other network items that may try to access your computer. These items can often be used for malicious means, but some of them have legitimate purposes.

Allowing ICMP traffic

An item you may sometimes wish to grant access through one of your firewall's doors is ICMP traffic. Whilst you don't need to know the full details of what ICMP traffic does, it is worth knowing that it is useful for some troubleshooting tasks on a network.

Let's grant incoming "pings" access through our firewall. ICMP pings are small "packets" of data that allow network support staff to discover if specific devices are attached to the network. If the firewall is blocking the ICMP ping, then a member of network personnel cannot tell if a computer is active on a network or not.

Beware

Whilst ICMP traffic can prove invaluable in troubleshooting PC network problems, it can also be exploited by hackers and malicious programs. Therefore, you should always remember to block it again through your firewall when you no longer need it.

93

1 Click Start, Control Panel, and double-click Administrative Tools

2 Double-click "Windows Firewall with Advanced Security"

🔐 Windows Firewall with Advanced Security

3 Click Continue at the User Account Control warning

4 Click the Windows Firewall Properties link

➡ Windows Firewall Properties

5 Click the IPsec Settings tab, and adjust the "Exempt ICMP from IPsec" setting to Yes. Click OK and close all windows to finish. When you no longer need ICMP ping access, remember to follow the same steps to block it again, adjusting the setting back to the default of No

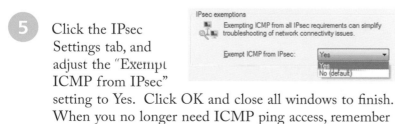

...cont'd

Activating the Windows Firewall security log

If you want to have a closer look at what the firewall is doing, you can activate the Windows Firewall security log.

1 Click Start, Control Panel, and double-click Administrative Tools

2 Double-click "Windows Firewall with Advanced Security", and click Continue at the User Account Control warning. Click the Windows Firewall Properties link

3 In the Logging section, click Customize...

4 Tick the "Log dropped packets" and "Log successful connections" check boxes.

5 Click OK, and then close all windows used

6 To examine the log file, launch Notepad by clicking the Start button, All Programs, Accessories, and Notepad

7 Once Notepad has launched, click File, and Open..., and in the "File name" field, type "c:\Windows\system32\LogFiles\Firewall\pfirewall.log", ensuring the file-type dropdown box is set to All Files. Click Open to view the log

Hot tip
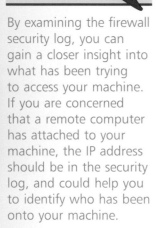

By examining the firewall security log, you can gain a closer insight into what has been trying to access your machine. If you are concerned that a remote computer has attached to your machine, the IP address should be in the security log, and could help you to identify who has been onto your machine.

Hot tip

Before you can read the firewall security log, you may need to grant yourself access to the file, using the skills learned in chapter 5, "Security for users".

Testing your security level

If you've followed all of the advice in this book so far, your PC should be a long way down the road towards tight security. In particular, since we've just been through a number of steps to secure our online security, we should be well protected against threats that occur via the Internet.

It's often difficult to measure the "success" of the security steps you have taken. Does the fact that you haven't had any security incidents mean that your security is watertight, or have you simply "got lucky"?

Fortunately, you can run some tests to see how strong your online PC security is, and it needn't cost you anything. Let's use the ShieldsUP! online security test to see if our security measures are working effectively.

1 Open Internet Explorer and visit www.grc.com/default, and scroll down to click the ShieldsUP! link

2 Read the information carefully and then click the Proceed button

3 The main ShieldsUP! page appears. There are a number of services that you can run

...cont'd

Hot tip

The ShieldsUP! page and the www.grc.com page in general contain some excellent security information, and it's worth taking some time to browse through to enhance your understanding of PC security requirements.

Don't forget

ShieldsUP! is an excellent service for testing your online security, and the tests we have conducted report that we are invisible on the Internet, which is the ideal status for us. Remember that PC security is wide-ranging though, and not all threats arrive via the Internet, and that the other security measures outlined in this book still require your attention.

Hot tip

It's worth trying the other tests on the ShieldsUP! services page too.

4   You can run the lower two tests if you want to test a specific port, but we are more interested in the generic tests on the upper gray bar. Click the File Sharing button, which will examine if remote computers can connect to our machine's ports for the purpose of collecting data from our file system

5   ShieldsUP! will run the test as requested, which may take a few minutes, and then present the results

6   The test results show that our machine is using stealth mode on some of the most important ports, and all attempts to collect information from the machine failed. ShieldsUP! rates our machine as "VERY SECURE"

7   Now scroll down the page and click the All Service Ports button, which conducts a more thorough port scan

8   Again, our PC has passed the test! This is great news for our online security, and lends us some peace of mind, too

8 Email security

Email systems are abused by viruses, spyware, hackers, phishers, and other PC threats as a channel to carry out their malicious work. Consequently, it stands to reason that you need to keep your email system safe and secure. By applying some security measures, utilizing some security tools, and throwing in some vigilance and restraint, you can make sure that your mailbox is another security hole plugged.

98 Understanding email security

99 What is phishing?

100 Identifying phishing

102 Dealing with phishing

103 Reporting phishing attempts

104 The Vista phishing filter

105 Marking an email legitimate

106 Junk email

108 Deterring junk email

109 Using an external junk filter

110 Windows Mail junk filter

111 Setting a protection level

112 Adding safe senders

114 Blocking senders

116 More mail security options

117 Using plain text

118 Using rules

120 Testing our message rule

Understanding email security

Early computer messaging programs simply passed plain text between computers. This meant that it was almost impossible for malicious programs to use the medium for their wrongdoings. The only malicious element of email in the early days was likely to be the words themselves!

Criminals hadn't seen any potential in email as a channel to execute their crimes, and so didn't exploit the systems for this purpose. The main vulnerability was that email systems didn't use a method known as encryption to "scramble" the text passing between users, and an advanced computer user could potentially intercept the text within the message.

What has changed?

Whilst modern email systems don't use encryption by default, they do now offer encryption as an option. Furthermore, greater barriers are available to prevent the intrusion of threats such as phishing, viruses, trojan horses, worms, and junk email.

Let's have another quick look at these threats to email systems.

Phishing

Phishing attempts use email messages in an effort to extract personal information from you, with the intention of using this information for criminal gain, such as identity fraud. We'll be looking at phishing more closely on the next page.

Viruses, trojan horses, and worms

Viruses, trojan horses, and worms can travel across email systems as attachments. When you innocently open the attachment, the malicious program attempts to infect your system.

Junk email

Although seemingly more irritating than anything else, we'll be looking at how junk email can slow your machine's performance, clog your mail box, and introduce security risks.

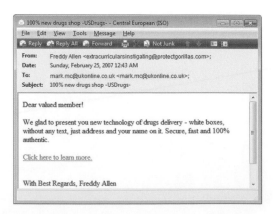

What is phishing?

Just as a fisherman drops his hook into the water hoping that a fish will take the bait, a "phishing" attempt uses the idea that if enough innocent people are targeted, a certain number of these will also "take the bait". "Phishers", the perpetrators of this crime, predominantly use emails that masquerade as genuine messages in order to deceptively extract personal details from people. These details are then commonly used for criminal purposes, whether these be selling the details on to other criminals, or abusing the details for monetary gain.

A common example

A large percentage of phishing attempts use banking systems as the facade for their fraudulent activity. In the example below, the phishing attempt purports to be from the Nationwide Bank, and asks the user to log in and confirm their account details.

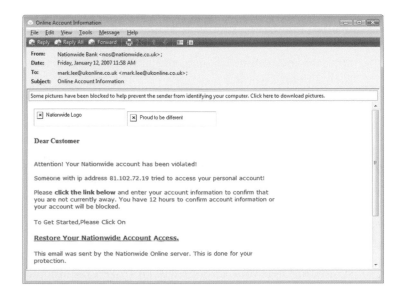

Hot tip

Without security in place, a message would have the bank's branding and images surrounding the text. However, Windows Mail hides the images by default, as the download of images can alert the phisher to the fact that you have received the message, and they may be able to identify your computer.

Should a recipient unquestioningly follow the instructions, it would be likely to result in the following actions:

- The recipient follows the link to a website, which is actually on a server owned by the phisher, designed to capture details

- The recipient enters their personal details into the web page

- The phisher captures and either sells or illegally uses the details

Identifying phishing

Whilst these guidelines are a good foundation to use for identifying phishing attempts, remember that criminals will always create new methods and tricks. Scrutinize suspect email messages carefully.

Let's break down the previous phishing example, to understand how we can identify that it is actually a phishing attempt. Armed with that knowledge, we can then learn how to deal with it.

1 Are you a customer of the purported sender? Many phishing efforts can be eliminated almost immediately. Do you even bank with Nationwide?

2 Does it look credible? Despite their continued efforts, many phishing emails are crudely worded and littered with spelling errors. In our example, the English used is often poor, using unusual phrases such as "your Nationwide account has been violated". Banks use accurate and careful English, and are unlikely to release such a poorly worded message

Attention! Your Nationwide account has been violated!

3 Is the message asking for personal details? Remember, banks and building societies never ask for account details over email. Never submit this information

4 Phishing attempts often use scare tactics, in an effort to trick people into making quick decisions. Is the message suggesting that your account will be frozen imminently, or that somebody else has been using your account? Be wary of such suggestions, and if you suspect your account security has been compromised, contact your bank

Please **click the link below** and enter your account information to confirm that you are not currently away. You have 12 hours to confirm account information or your account will be blocked.

5 Hover the mouse over any links you are asked to follow, and check the displayed address at the foot of the message, which displays where the link is actually pointing to. In our example, the link in the message states it will open a web page at the Nationwide site, but hovering the mouse over the link reveals the true destination, www.bio-therapy.net/media/index.html

Beware

While hovering over the link and reading the web address, notice that phishers often select web addresses that look, at first glance, like a legitimate, existing web address.

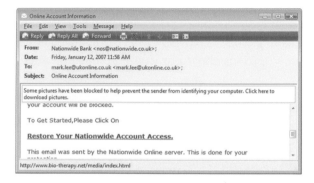

6 Just as web links can be misleading, so too can email address links. A process known as "spoofing" is used by phishers, as well as other unscrupulous email users, to make the message recipient believe that they are sending return messages to a perfectly legitimate email address. As with web links, you can also hover over email address links to discover their true destination

7 Has the Windows Mail phishing filter placed the suspect email into the "Junk E-mail" folder? We'll be looking at the "Junk E-mail" folder later in the chapter

Beware

Windows will not pick out every single phishing attempt. You need to understand phishing and its characteristics to be able to identify it for yourself.

8 Always maintain a common-sense approach to email correspondence. Never make snap decisions, never enter any personal details unless you are totally sure of authenticity, and if in any doubt at all, discard the email completely

Dealing with phishing

Just as gaining an appreciation of how criminals operate makes you better able to protect yourself and your home, understanding how phishing emails work lends us the ability to arm ourselves against such opportunist attacks.

Let's look at some basic rules on how to deal with phishing. After that, we'll investigate how we can report phishing attempts, and then go on to explore the Vista phishing filter.

1. Confirm that your identification is correct by running a search on the Internet. A quick search on the anti-phishing website phishery.internetdefence.net confirms our suspicions about our example phishing email

2. Do not reply. Doing so confirms your email address, and provides a trail for the phisher to work upon

3. Never follow the links provided on the website, even if you are curious to see where they lead

4. Windows Mail hides images in email messages by default. Keep this setting enabled, and don't click the link to download images. Displaying images can help the phisher to locate and identify your machine

Some pictures have been blocked to help prevent the sender from identifying your computer. Click here to download pictures.

Reporting phishing attempts

It's important in the battle against phishing to report attempts made against you; after all, phishing is a criminal activity, and the sender probably wants to take your money from you, whether this is to be done directly or indirectly.

Fortunately, many sites contain instructions on reporting phishing. Let's see how we can report a phishing attempt to eBay, following a message purporting to be from the famous auction website.

Beware

If you think your account details or any other banking information may have been compromised, you need to telephone your bank immediately.

1 Visit www.ebay.com and click the Security & Resolution Center link at the foot of the page

| Security & Resolution Center |

2 Select the "Spoof (fake) email" radio button and click Report Problem

⊙ **Spoof (fake) email** - You received a suspicious-looking email that appears to be from eBay or PayPal and you want eBay to take action.

3 Select "Spam, fake emails, and other email-related problems" from the Step 1 box, and then "Report an email from eBay that may be fake", before clicking Continue

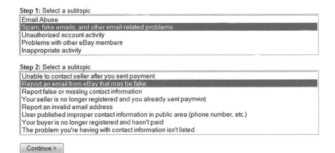

Step 1: Select a subtopic
Email Abuse
Spam, fake emails, and other email-related problems
Unauthorized account activity
Problems with other eBay members
Inappropriate activity

Step 2: Select a subtopic
Unable to contact seller after you sent payment
Report an email from eBay that may be fake
Report false or missing contact information
Your seller is no longer registered and you already sent payment
Report an invalid email address
User published improper contact information in public area (phone number, etc.)
Your buyer is no longer registered and hasn't paid
The problem you're having with contact information isn't listed

Continue >

Hot tip

As well as instructing you on how to report phishing emails, the eBay Security & Resolution Center also contains some useful phishing and spoof-email information.

4 eBay instructs you on how to report phishing attempts to them. You need to forward the message to spoof@ebay.com. Use Windows Mail to do so

Hot tip

You can also forward phishing and spoof PayPal emails. Use spoof@paypal.com.

7. **Educate yourself on how to recognize and <u>report spoof email</u> and <u>Web sites impersonating eBay</u>.** The most common way for an eBay account to be compromised is through spoof emails designed to access members' passwords and other sensitive information. Please forward any suspicious or unexpected emails claiming to be from eBay to us at the email address spoof@ebay.com. It's also a good idea to review the <u>Spoof Tutorial</u> and other online security information available from the eBay <u>Security and Resolution Center</u>. Also, consider <u>installing the eBay Toolbar</u> to take advantage of the eBay Toolbar <u>Account Guard</u>.

The Vista phishing filter

From what we've looked at so far, it's clear that phishing is a real security threat on modern PCs, and something with which we need to exercise due vigilance.

Microsoft has recognized the threat that phishing poses, and developed a phishing filter that is integrated into Windows Mail.

Let's have a look at how to use it.

1 Launch Windows Mail, click Tools on the menu bar, and then choose Junk E-mail Options…

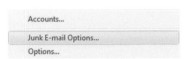

2 Click on the Phishing tab, to review the phishing filter options

3 Ensure that both options have ticks in the check boxes. If not, place a tick inside. This will ensure that your incoming mail is protected from phishing messages, and also that any suspected phishing emails are moved to the Junk Mail folder, which reduces the chance of phishing emails being mistaken amongst the genuine messages

Marking an email legitimate

It's quite possible that the phishing filter could identify some perfectly legitimate email messages as phishing attempts. The phishing filter allows you to mark messages as legitimate that it has initially flagged as suspect.

In this example, there is a message in the inbox that has been marked as suspect, but of which we trust the sender.

1 Click the email you wish to mark as legitimate, and note the message that Windows Mail has placed at the top of the preview pane

Hot tip

Once you've unblocked a message that the phishing filter marked as suspect, you may also want to click the header to enable images, as in our example. Remain cautious, and make sure you trust the sender.

105

2 Click the Unblock button to the right of the message in the preview pane to mark the message as legitimate

3 Note the links are now active in the message, and it returns to standard black text

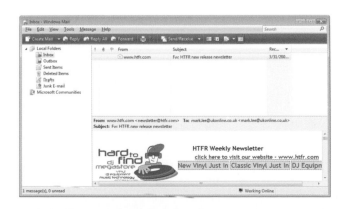

Junk email

We've come across the term "junk email" in this chapter, and as we've noticed, the phishing filter can automatically send detected phishing attempts to the "Junk E-mail" folder.

What is junk email?

Junk email, sometimes referred to as UCE (Unsolicited Commercial Email), UBE (Unsolicited Bulk Email) or simply as "Spam", is similar in principle to the unsolicited junk mail you receive in your home mailbox. The difference is that junk email costs you as the recipient, in terms of disk storage, processing, delivery costs (in terms of your Internet connection), and, of course, your time spent dealing with it!

Volume and types of junk email

Junk email is now a huge problem; it is estimated that in June 2006, 55 billion junk email messages were sent every day! Due to its substantial volume it clogs up mailboxes across the world, and necessitates entire systems to deal with it, not to mention the time spent by individuals. Junk email persists because it is a cheap option for the perpetrators, a fraction of the cost of the same direct marketing approach via the normal mail system.

Identifying a junk email message

No junk email utility is able to identify every piece of junk email, and since spammers are continually developing cunning methods of evading easy identification, it's beneficial for you as a user to be able to identify a junk email message for yourself. Let's use a real example, and examine its characteristics:

Consider the following email:

106

There are a number of clues in our sample email that can quickly lead us to the conclusion that it is unsolicited commercial email.

1 The email message is extremely unprofessional. It contains spelling errors (note the use of "Aggresive" and "guaranted"), it's badly formatted, the grammar is poor, and the language inappropriate

2 The sender is not known to the recipient. This could be from a username harvested by the spammers, or it could be a randomly generated name "spoofed" to conceal the real identity of the sender. Of course, it could also be the email address of an unwitting user whose PC is being abused for this purpose

3 The message text contains words deliberately spelled to avoid detection by junk email filters. In this example, the word "symbol" is represented as "Sym8oL":

Sym8oL: **CCTI**

4 There is no company name on the message, so who stands to benefit from telling you about this? Why would somebody who has "guaranteed" knowledge of a coming lucrative trading opportunity wish to tell you?

5 The message simply lacks credibility. It claims that a company's share price is about to rocket, and that if you invest, you will gain a "guaranteed" 500% profit. Stock and share behavior is, of course, never guaranteed, and 500% is an extremely unrealistic figure

500% profit guaranted, it's progressive company!!!

6 The message is promoting the investment of stocks or shares. Some of the most popular subjects of junk email include prescription drugs, pornography, loan and mortgage offers, replica brand goods, pirated software, and penny stocks

Beware

Watch out for junk email such as this encouraging you to urgently purchase stocks and shares. These are almost invariably "pump and dump" frauds, where spammers attempt to raise the price of a stock through this type of marketing and promotion. This practice is illegal. Do not be tempted!

Hot tip

Did you notice that the subject of the message seemed to be random? It most probably is. Spammers use randomly generated subjects in an attempt to evade junk email filters that filter using the subject text.

Deterring junk email

It's a difficult fact to accept that you can't really do much to prevent junk email from reaching and cluttering up your inbox on a daily basis. It's an irritating element of modern computing that will most likely be with us for the foreseeable future.

That said, there are some measures you can take to help deter junk email. Alternatively, if you are upset by some junk email you've received, there is some work you can do against it.

Minimizing and deterring junk email

Let's look at some steps we can take to minimize the level of junk email we receive

1. Give out your email address carefully. Spammers are always hunting for valid email addresses

2. Avoid posting your email address on message boards and forums unless strictly necessary. These areas are a treasure trove for spammers looking to harvest quality addresses

3. As we've discussed already, you should never reply to junk email, even if it is to unsubscribe or raise a complaint

4. Ask people not to include your name in the "To" or "CC" lists when they forward emails on. A list like this is a treat for spammers

5. Follow the other recommendations in this book. For instance, installing antispyware, antivirus software, and a firewall will help you avoid becoming a zombie or "bot"

6. Employ some email filtering. We'll be looking at filtering next, and then message rules later in the chapter

Taking the fight to the spammers

If you are determined to fight against the junk email you receive, which has most probably been sent illegally, you can try to trace the origin of the message from the IP address. Spammers are unable to change the original IP address visible in the message source. In our example, the message originates from Russia.

Beware

If you are determined to battle against the junk email you receive, be aware that spammers are constantly moving and changing, and very difficult to trace. Tracking the origins of an email is difficult, but doing some work on investigating a junk email message will be, if nothing else, a good learning experience.

Using an external junk filter

Another option in the war against junk email is to employ the services of an external junk email filter. Whilst Windows Mail has a new junk email filter that we will be looking at shortly, there is another option which is also worth taking advantage of.

Using Mailwasher

Mailwasher is a junk email prevention and filtering application. The way it differs from some other anti-junk-email systems is that it can block junk emails on the mail server itself, so that the message never reaches your PC. Since spammers take advantage of features within PC email clients to trace whether you have opened the message, it's useful to have a tool that prevents these messages from ever touching your PC.

How does it work?

Mailwasher works by reading your emails directly from your Internet service provider's server, without downloading them to your email program. You can delete junk email on the email server from within Mailwasher, and you can even set a "bounceback" message that tells the spammer your address is not a valid one, in the hope that your address may be removed from the spammer's list. It's actually unlikely that they are organized and meticulous enough to do this, and your bounceback message may go to an address they have spoofed, but you may consider it worth trying.

Hot tip

"Bouncing" a junk email back to a spammer is the electronic equivalent of sending some junk mail back to the originating company with a note to say "address not found". It indicates to the spammer that they are wasting their time using your email address.

Beware

Junk email, as with phishing attempts, often has code embedded that tries to send a message to the spammer to inform them that you have read the message. Windows Mail doesn't display images by default, to help prevent this type of activity.

Bounce	Delete	Status	Size	From	Subject	Sent	Account
			1.5KB	Kaarle DeSouza (kaarle...	Abwesenheitsnotiz.	28 May 2	Freenetname
			30.6KB	Hasina1997 (bachewic...	Countless men have passed through the l...	28 May 2	Freenetname
			31.1KB	maureus1995 (maureus...	You get a series of documents named PC ...	28 May 2	Freenetname
			24.6KB	markhuu1995 (markhuu...	The Chicken did not appear to be in a par...	28 May 2	Freenetname
			1.5KB	Jf minami (minami@rdm...	Add, to your radar.	28 May 2	Freenetname
			3.1KB	Louis Pasteur (hwygzogi...	anlagerichtlinien	28 May 2	Freenetname
			21.5KB	juliana2000 (janzenxufe...	But my real accomplishment came later.	28 May 2	Freenetname
			1.1KB	jun DeSouza (desouza...	Exchange news.	28 May 2	Freenetname
			26.3KB	Larry1999 (larryrg@asso...	If the function succeeds, the return value ...	28 May 2	Freenetname
			20.7KB	sardescu2003 (sardesc...	Each device is identified by a major numb...	28 May 2	Freenetname

Check Mail · Stop · Process Mail · Mail Program · Spam Tools

Mail was last checked 1 minute ago — Cancel

Other options

Mailwasher and other junk filters have other useful options in the battle against junk email. You can create blacklists specifying usernames and domain names of spammers, and set up your own rules to automatically filter emails. We'll be looking at this type of functionality within Windows Mail.

Windows Mail junk filter

As we have seen, Windows Vista has been designed by Microsoft to be a secure system to work with. One of the major new features is the junk email filter, which is there to help you deal with the increasing amounts of spam, junk, and phishing attempts.

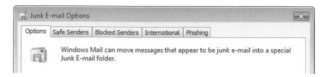

The "Junk E-mail" folder

Windows Mail contains a new folder called "Junk E-mail", which you will remember from the section dealing with phishing attempts, covered earlier in the chapter.

The "Junk E-mail" folder is a holding area for all suspicious messages. Windows Mail moves messages it believes to be "junk" into this folder according to various criteria and the level of protection that you choose to implement.

Protection level

The junk email filter protection level tells Windows Mail how you would like suspicious emails to be dealt with.

There are four protection levels available for you to choose from:

- *No Automatic Filtering*. With this setting enabled, no junk email is moved into the junk email folder unless the sender appears in your "blocked senders" list

- *Low*. This is the default level, and with this enabled, obvious junk email is moved to the junk email folder

- *High*. The junk email filter is more severe in its selection of suspected junk emails when this setting is enabled

- *Safe List Only*. With this setting enabled, you will only receive mail to your inbox from people or domains who feature on your Safe Senders List

Hot tip

Remember to check the "Junk E-mail" folder regularly. There is always a possibility that perfectly legitimate messages have been mistakenly identified as "junk" and placed into this folder.

Hot tip

The "Safe List Only" protection level will provide some help against viruses and other threats that arrive via email, as viruses often use random or harvested email addresses. Of course, the possibility always remains that a virus may arrive from a friend's email address, so stay alert.

Setting a protection level

Windows Vista is designed to be secure and flexible, and the junk email filter is a good example of these two requirements working together. You as a user can pick and choose the right level of protection according to the way you use your machine.

What type of email user are you?

The level of protection you choose will depend upon what type of user you are. Do you send and receive an average volume of mail? If so, you may want the "Low" option, which moves the most obvious messages to the "Junk E-mail" folder. Do you receive email from a carefully selected group of people, and never wish to receive mail from others outside of this group? Take advantage of the "Safe List Only" option, which will only deliver messages from people or domains you have specified in your Safe Senders List.

Let's see how we can adjust the protection level.

Hot tip

We'll be looking at how to add people and domains to the Safe Senders List in the next section.

1 In Windows Mail, select Tools and Junk E-mail Options... from the menu bar

2 Adjust the radio button to the protection level you would like to use and click OK

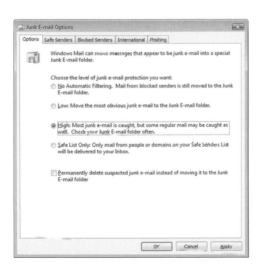

Beware

Exercise caution when deciding whether to use the "Permanently delete suspected junk e-mail..." check box. It's impossible for Windows Mail to make the correct decision on junk email every single time, so there's a potential that you could lose genuine messages.

You are now protected by the level of security imposed by your chosen protection level. If your chosen level proves to be either too stringent, or not stringent enough, you can always make an adjustment to it later.

Adding safe senders

Hot tip

Adding a domain to the Safe Senders List means that any messages arriving from people with an email address at the same domain are automatically set as "safe". So, for example, if you added computerstep.co.uk to the Safe Senders List, an email from john@ computerstep.co.uk would arrive in your inbox and be ignored by the junk email filter.

In our examination of the various protection levels offered by the junk email filter, we've seen the Safe Senders List mentioned. The Safe Senders List identifies senders that you trust, and whose messages you want to make sure don't end up in the "Junk E-mail" folder.

Not only is the Safe Senders List a very useful tool for all email users, but it is essential if you have chosen the "Safe List Only" protection level. If you were to set your protection level to "Safe List Only", and didn't make any entries in the Safe Senders List, all of your received emails would end up in your "Junk E-mail" folder!

There are two ways to add users to the Safe Senders List. Let's have a look at both.

From the inbox

It is possible to add users and domains to the Safe Senders List directly from the inbox or any sub-folder, if you have a message from the user available.

1. In the Windows Mail inbox, right-click a message from the sender, and select "Junk E-mail", followed by "Add Sender to Safe Senders List"

> Add Sender to Safe Senders List
> Add Sender's Domain to Safe Senders List

2. Windows Mail confirms the sender has been added to the list

Adding users to the Safe Senders List by this method is handy if you want to build up your list of trusted senders on an ad hoc basis. If you want to take a more methodical route to the construction of your Safe Senders List, use the Junk E-mail Options.

From within the Junk E-mail Options

OK, let's take a look at how to manually add users to the Safe Senders List within the Junk E-mail Options. This option will be useful to you if you have a predefined collection of addresses you wish to add to your Safe Senders List.

1 In Windows Mail, click Tools, then Junk E-mail Options..., and select the Safe Senders tab

2 Click the Add... button, and in the window that appears, enter the email address you wish to add to the Safe Senders List

3 When complete, click the OK button, and then OK again to return to the inbox

113

Blocking senders

Just as the Windows Mail Junk E-mail Options include a method of marking users and domains as safe, via the Safe Senders List, you also have the opportunity to block senders.

If you add a sender or a domain to your Blocked Senders List, Windows Mail treats any messages from the sender (or the domain, if you have specified one) as junk email and will automatically move them directly to the Junk E-Mail folder.

As with the Safe Senders List, there are two different ways to add senders and domains to the Blocked Senders List. Let's start by adding a sender to the list from directly inside the inbox.

From the inbox

The process for adding a user to the Blocked Senders List is almost the same as for adding a user to the Safe Senders List. It is this kind of consistent design that enables easy administration of your email within Windows Mail.

1 In the Windows Mail inbox, right-click a message from the sender, and select "Junk E-mail", followed by "Add Sender to Blocked Senders List"

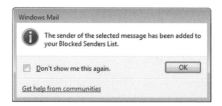

2 Windows Mail confirms that the sender has been added to the Blocked Senders List

3 Click the check box if you don't wish to see the confirmation message each time you add an address to the Blocked Senders List, and click OK to finish

Hot tip

Click the "Don't show me this again" check box on the confirmation message if you don't want to see confirmation of a sender added to the Safe Senders or Blocked Senders lists every time.

From within the Junk E-mail Options

Let's see how we manually add senders to the Blocked Senders List within the Junk E-mail Options.

1 Launch the Windows Mail program, click Tools on the menu bar, click Junk E-mail Options..., and then select the Blocked Senders tab

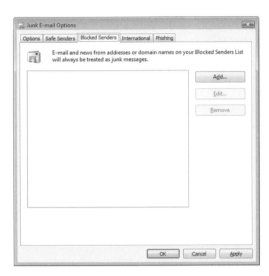

Hot tip

If you ever need to review and adjust your lists of safe and blocked senders, from within Windows Mail select Tools, and Junk E-mail Options.... Choose the appropriate Senders tab (Safe or Blocked), and you can edit and remove entries as required.

2 Click Add..., and in the window that appears, enter the email address, or domain, you wish to add to the Blocked Senders List. When finished, click OK and OK again to return to the inbox

Don't forget

Spammers often use stolen and harvested email addresses, and change them every time they send a new batch, so blocking individual spammers may prove largely fruitless. Blocking senders is more useful for repeat junk email offenders.

Messages arriving from the email addresses you've added to your Blocked Senders List will now be treated as junk email by Windows Mail.

More mail security options

It is worth taking a few moments to review some of the other security options featured in Windows Mail that we haven't covered so far, and considering whether the default choices are the right ones for you.

There are some more options located in the Security tab of the Options window.

Hot tip

Although we don't have the space here, it is worth reading up on all of these security options when you have some time. The default options provide a good level of security, but it is useful to know the effects that changing this security level, in whichever direction, will have upon the usability and functionality of Windows Mail.

1 In Windows Mail, click Tools on the menu bar, and choose Options…

2 Click the Security tab

Beware

Unless you have a very specific reason, it's advisable to leave the "Do not allow attachments …" option enabled. Many viruses use email attachments to do their work, and you should never open an attachment unless you are certain what it is and whom it is from.

- Virus Protection and security zone. This is a useful option, as it integrates the security zones we looked at in chapter 7 into Windows Mail. Be aware that security changes you make in Internet Explorer affect the security in Windows Mail

- "Do not allow attachments…". Whilst you won't be able to use some attachments, this is a great safeguard against viruses

- Download Images. It is advisable to leave the "Block images …" option enabled, as some parties can tell if you have read an email by embedding images in a message

Using plain text

Frequently, securing your PC can involve a trade-off between functionality and security. Using plain text in your email application is an example of this in action. Whilst the content available within an email message has become enhanced and more sophisticated over the years, it has also introduced the potential for the abuse of these enhanced features.

Plain text versus HTML

Early incarnations of email applications used plain text only. As the World Wide Web gained in popularity and HTML became the standard language for web pages, email programs began to allow the use of HTML within messages. Whilst this provides a wealth of display options and flexibility for the sender, it can also allow the introduction of security issues. For this reason, you may prefer to send and receive your messages in plain text only.

Reading and sending messages in plain text

Let's set all of our received messages, and all of the messages we send, to automatically default to plain text.

1 In Windows Mail, click Tools, and then Options…

2 Click the Read tab, and place a tick in the check box next to "Read all messages in plain text"

> ☑ Automatically <u>d</u>ownload message when viewing in the Preview Pane
> ☑ <u>R</u>ead all messages in plain text
> ☑ S<u>h</u>ow ToolTips in the message list for clipped items

3 With the Options window still open, click the Send tab

4 Adjust the radio button below Mail Sending Format to Plain Text

> Mail Sending Format
> ○ <u>H</u>TML   [HTML Settings…]   [Plain Text Settings…]
> ◉ Plain Text

5 Click OK to close the Options window

Using rules

Do you want to make sure that all emails containing an attachment go to a specific folder, so that you can review them later in one place? Would you like to send all messages containing the word "medications" in the subject field to the "Junk E-mail" folder? Or perhaps you'd like to automatically delete all emails from a certain sender? If so, message rules are for you. Let's try setting one up.

Creating a message rule

Spammers frequently use numbers or other characters in place of letters in an effort to avoid junk email filters. For example, they may use a carefully placed zero in the word "mortgage", to create a combination of letters that, to the human eye, looks the same. Our rule is going to automatically send messages with "m0rtgage" in the subject line to the "Junk E-mail" folder.

1 In Windows Mail, on the menu bar, click Tools, Message Rules, Mail…, and then the New… button

2 Firstly, we have to specify the conditions for the rule. The condition we want to meet is that the subject line contains the word "m0rtgage", so place a tick in the "Where the Subject line contains specific words" check box

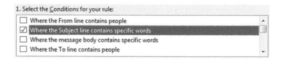

3 In section 3 of the new mail rule, you'll notice that a link has appeared. Click the "contains specific words" link, type in the desired word (in this case "m0rtgage"), click Add, and finally click OK

Hot tip

As you build your message rule, observe the way that the rule description develops in section 3 of the window.

4 Next, in section 2 of the rule, we need to tell Windows Mail the action we would like it to take once the condition is met. So what should it do if "m0rtgage" appears in the Subject line? Click the check box next to "Move it to the specified folder"

5 Just as we specified the details of the condition, we also need to specify the details of the action. Click the new link that has appeared in section 3, entitled "specified"

6 Select the "Junk E-mail" folder from your list of Windows Mail folders, and then click OK

7 Type a name for your rule in section 4 of the New Mail Rule window

8 Click OK to complete the construction of your message rule. You can then review it in the Message Rules list

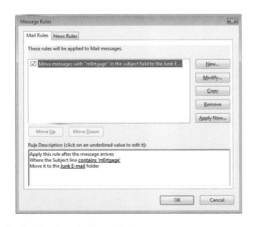

Beware

Message rules are a real advantage in the battle against junk email. Be aware, however, that spammers are ever more devious and imaginative, and with that in mind it will never be possible to write a rule against every possible junk email. The best mind-set to adopt is to aim to target the repeal offenders.

119

Testing our message rule

In the last steps, we created a message rule that filters out emails with the word "m0rtgage" in the subject line, and takes the action of moving the message to the "Junk E-mail" folder. It would be reassuring to know that the rule does actually pick up the messages we want it to, so let's run a quick test.

Don't forget

Even though we are sending our test email to our own email address, it still takes the same journey via our ISP's server and back, as other external messages would, and is therefore a good way to test the message rule.

Hot tip

Did your test message come back at all? If you have spam filtering for your mailbox enabled at your ISP, it may have been picked up by their own spam filter!

1 In Windows Mail, start a new message by clicking the Create Mail button

2 Address it to your own email address, and in the subject line, type "m0rtgage"

3 Click the Send button, and then the Send/Receive button in the main Windows Mail window

4 Check the "Junk E-mail" folder, and the test message should have been successfully moved inside by our message rule

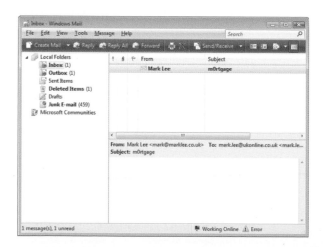

9 Securing your network

Ever since personal computers have joined networks, the security risks have increased. Fortunately, there are many steps you can take to protect your machine and its data.

122 Introducing network security

123 Early considerations

124 Password-protect the router

125 Using a WEP security key

126 Using a WPA security key

127 IP addresses

128 Setting static IP addresses

130 The router firewall

131 Preventing access by time

133 Control by MAC address

Introducing network security

As we've discussed in earlier chapters, the explosion of computer networking technology and its rapid implementation has transformed the way we use computers and our ability to share information.

As we've also seen, this has resulted in a similar rise in network security threats, and the resulting development of network security has been both huge and complex.

The good news

There is some good news, however.

- We've implemented a lot of security in this book so far against threats traveling across networks and the Internet

- Windows Vista is a very secure operating system, including its network security framework

- As a home PC user, your security issues won't be as vast as that of a corporate network security support person

Our chapters on virus security, Internet security and email security, and some of the forthcoming chapters, all describe security measures that prevent network- and Internet-based threats from accessing your PC.

Much of our focus in this chapter will have to be centered upon a new vulnerability that has occurred following a meteoric rise of a certain type of technology. Can you think what this could be?

Wireless networks

Wireless networks have transformed the way in which we can connect to corporate networks and to the Internet. Notebook users can now work on the Internet and access their corporate networks using technologies like Virtual Private Networking, or VPN for short. At home, people can link up their multiple PCs without having to string wires between them.

This new convenience has also brought security risks, too. Many people have wireless networks at home with no security configured, which means that "intruders" may be able to connect to your network. These intruders don't need to enter your home. They may be parked in your street, camped out in the field next to you, or sitting on their couch next door.

Early considerations

Connecting computers together on a network has always carried risks. When computers were connected together in a single room, with known, trusted people using the machines, the risk level was low.

As networks began to run across multiple rooms, through businesses and institutions, and across to multiple sites, the risks increased. The chances were that you couldn't physically see everyone using a computer on the network, and you had no chance of watching their entire computing time to see if they were to make mistakes or engage in malicious behavior that may threaten your computer security.

When the Internet arrived, the risks grew phenomenally. Suddenly, your computer could be connected to the largest network in the world, a truly frightening prospect!

Let's look at some basic considerations for implementing a network in today's vastly interconnected computing environment.

Move away from analog dial-up

Using a modem over a traditional phone line to dial up the Internet, in addition to all of the poor-performance issues, poses certain threats to your PC. Rogue dialers, as we looked at in chapter 7, are more able to exploit analog dial-up modems than broadband connections. You don't get the security benefits of a broadband router either.

Invest in a wireless router

If you are keen to "go wireless", pay a little extra to get a wireless router, rather than just a wireless modem. Implementing a router means that you have got an extra layer of security between your PC and the rest of the world, giving you enhanced protection against malicious intruders and software. Most routers include a firewall for additional security.

Implement a key to prevent unauthorized access

Many wireless networks are vulnerable to piggybacking, where other people access your wireless connection to surf the web without your knowledge. They may also engage in "war driving", which is the practice of locating unsecured wireless networks by driving around a neighborhood with a wireless-enabled notebook. You must implement a key to block this, as we shall see.

Beware

You must enable a key on your wireless network. People piggybacking onto your connection will slow your performance, and they may use your connection for illegitimate purposes.

Password-protect the router

Hot tip

If people are able to successfully "ping" you across the Internet, they only get as far as your router, not your PC. Just as we saw that Windows Firewall blocks "pings", we will also be looking at how to block pings to our router.

Let's look at securing a wireless network configuration using the solid option of a wireless router with an integral firewall. We can't hope to cover the variety of wireless routers on the market, so the following steps have been completed using a Belkin ADSL modem with Wireless-G router. Whilst the settings will be similar across products, you should refer to your router's manual and the manufacturer if you need further information.

The first step we need to take is to secure access to our router's configuration with an administrator password.

1 Launch an Internet Explorer window and type in the address to your router's setup page. This is often set to a default of 192.168.2.1. Check your manual if unsure

Hot tip

Routers use a web browser interface for you to be able to adjust settings.

2 If a password hasn't been set already, this field may be blank. Check your router manual for confirmation. Click Submit to log in

Hot tip

If you manage to lock yourself out of your router, or if you make errors during setup that you are unable to undo, most devices have a small reset button that you can use to return to the factory defaults.

3 Click the System Settings link at the bottom left of the window

4 Type in a new password of appropriate complexity in both fields, and click Apply Changes

Administrator Password:
The Router ships with NO password entered. If you wish to add a password for more security, you can set a password here. More Info

Type in current Password >

Type in new Password >   ●●●●●●●●●●

Confirm new Password >   ●●●●●●●●●●

Login Timeout >   10   (1-99 minutes)

Using a WEP security key

It's difficult to exaggerate the importance of protecting access to your wireless router. Resulting in potential performance problems at best, and individuals surfing for dubious material under your broadband connection or eavesdropping on your communications at worst, unsecured wireless access is rarely of benefit to you.

Remember, wireless routers have strong signal ranges, so there may be many people who can locate your wireless network.

Fortunately, implementing security on your wireless router does not take long, but the benefits will last you a long time. Let's set a WEP security key for our router, so that anyone connecting to our router as an "access point" will need to enter a phrase of our choosing.

1　Launch Internet Explorer and log in to the router setup utility again, using the password we set in the last steps

2　In the Wireless section on the left side, click the Security link

Channel and SSID
Security
Wireless Bridge

3　Adjust the Allowed Client Type drop-down list to WEP

WEP ▼
Disabled
WEP
WPA/WPA2
WPA2 Only

4　Ensure that the WEP mode is set to 128 bit. You can now enter either a 26-digit code (using a format known as hexadecimal), or you can enter a passphrase of your choice which the utility will convert into a 26-digit hex code for you. Enter a phrase into the Passphrase field, tick the check box, and click Apply Changes

Key 1 >	
Key 2 >	
Key 3 >	
Key 4 >	
Default Key ID >	1 ▾
Passphrase >	☑ a_very_complex_password

5　Click Logout to exit. When you want to attach other devices to your wireless network, you will need to enter this generated passphrase or "key"

Hot tip

WEP keys provide a good level of security, but if you have devices that are confirmed to support the more advanced WPA security, use that instead, as there are some tools that can break through WEP security. We will be looking at setting a WPA key next.

Hot tip

Hexadecimal is a number system that uses a combination of numerals between 0 and 9, and the letters A to F. If you are not familiar with hexadecimal, then it's easiest to use a phrase and allow the system to convert it for you.

Don't forget

Any trusted users who want to connect to your wireless network will need to enter the passphrase when requested.

Using a WPA security key

Implementing a WEP key is a good start on the journey to wireless network security, but if the devices you use to connect to your wireless network can support WPA, it is a far more secure option to adopt. It is no more difficult to implement than a WEP key.

Let's set one now.

1 Open up an Internet Explorer window, visit your router setup page as before, and log in

2 Click the Security link on the left, in the Wireless section

Channel and SSID
Security
Wireless Bridge

3 Adjust the Allowed Client Type drop-down list setting to WPA/WPA2

WEP ▼
Disabled
WEP
WPA/WPA2
WPA2 Only

4 Ensure Authentication is set to "Pre-shared Key"

Authentication >   ○ 802.1X ● Pre-shared Key

5 Enter a passphrase in the "Pre-shared Key" field. This should be suitably complex and must be at least eight characters long

Allowed Client Type >	WPA/WPA2 ▾
Authentication >	○ 802.1X ● Pre-shared Key
Encryption Technique >	AES ▾
Pre-shared Key >	••••••••

6 Click Apply Changes for the setting to take effect

7 Remember to log out of the setup utility when you have finished

Your router is now secured with the stronger WPA key. Anyone wishing to access your wireless network from another computer will need to enter the passphrase you have just set.

Hot tip

The Pre-Shared Key authentication type, sometimes shortened to PSK, is a method of implementing WPA security on a home network. The other available option, 802.1x, is designed for corporate environments where an 802.1x authentication server is required.

126

Don't forget

Use the password complexity rules we established in chapter 3 to ensure your passwords are suitably secure. Your passwords need to be unguessable and uncrackable!

IP addresses

You have probably heard of IP addresses before. Indeed, we've come across IP addresses in this book.

An IP address is a set of numbers to uniquely identify your machine on a network. Every machine participating in a TCP/IP network has to have a unique IP address for the duration of its stay on that network.

Private and public IP addresses

On your home network, you are free to choose which IP address you would like to use from a group of set ranges. On the Internet, you can only use addresses that have been allocated to you by your ISP.

The good news about this arrangement is that most Internet routers ignore any communications from private IP addresses, so it is very difficult for a hacker to attach to your PC over the Internet. As a consequence, many hacking attempts involve efforts to encourage you, either manually or via a program, to perform actions on your PC that "open up" your security doors.

Using DHCP

You can set your IP address manually, or you can use something called DHCP to automatically allocate an IP address to any computer that connects to your private network. Many routers come with an internal DHCP server to do this.

However, whilst a DHCP server is extremely useful, and almost indispensable for a large corporate network, it lowers your security considerably. If someone does manage to attach to your wireless network by discovering the key, the DHCP server will allocate them an IP address. If somebody connects a network cable into your router, it will allocate them an IP address. Let's disable the DHCP server on our router.

① Log into your router through Internet Explorer, as in the previous examples

② Click the LAN Settings link

LAN Setup
LAN Settings

③ Adjust the DHCP Server radio button to Off, if it isn't already, and click Apply Changes

Hot tip

In the corporate environment, DHCP performs other duties too, such as supplying IP address information about other servers.

Hot tip

You can use DHCP securely if you set up MAC address filtering. This takes some extra work, but we will be looking at using it later in the chapter.

Beware

Once you've disabled the DHCP server, every device requesting to attach to your network will need a static IP address in order to do so. We'll be looking at how to set a static IP address next.

Setting static IP addresses

If you have decided that you are going to disable DHCP on your home network, then it's a good step towards tighter security. You will need to spend some time allocating static IP addresses to any computer wishing to attach to your network, because the DHCP server will no longer be distributing IP addresses. The time you spend on this task should be a small price to pay in return for tighter security!

Choosing IP addresses

Your first consideration will be which IP address range you are going to use. For the purposes of this example, we're going to use a common default for compatibility purposes. You may want to consider using a different address "range" however, because doing so can add an extra layer of security.

Let's set a static IP address for our computer. We'll assume that your router is set to the standard IP address of 192.168.2.1, and that there are no other devices with IP addresses on your local network.

Before you start, you'll need to make a note of your DNS server IP addresses. If you are not sure what these are, check on your ISP's website, or contact them for help.

128

1 Click Start, and then choose Control Panel

2 Double-click the Network and Sharing Center icon

Network and Sharing Center

3 Click the "Manage network connections" link

Set up a connection or network
Manage network connections
Diagnose and repair

4 Double-click the network connection you use to connect to your router. If you have a standard configuration, it may be the only connection present

LAN or High-Speed Internet (1)

Local Area Connection
Home Network
SiS 900 PCI Fast Ethernet Ad...

5 A status window will appear with some handy
information about the connection

6 Click the Properties button

7 Click Continue at the User Account Control warning

8 A Properties window appears.
Double-click Internet Protocol
Version 4 (TCP/IPv4)

10 Enter the IP address
information as illustrated,
and enter the DNS
details you obtained
earlier from your
ISP. We are going to
use an IP address of
192.168.2.72

11 Click OK, OK again,
Close, and then close the
Network Connections
window. Close the Network and Sharing Center, and
finally Control Panel. You should now be able to access
your wireless network, knowing that you are using the
safer option of static addressing

129

The router firewall

The chances are that your wireless router will come with an integral firewall. A "hardware" firewall, such as one built in to a router, complements the work of your local software firewall. By blocking different types of security threat, the combination constructs a formidable barrier to malicious threats.

Additional features

Your firewall should offer you additional features and added security flexibility. Many of these features are worth taking advantage of. The firewall features that come with our chosen router that we are going to examine are:

● Preventing access via the router at certain times of day

● Control over which devices can access the router using MAC address filtering

Enabling the firewall

Firstly, we need to ensure that we are being protected by our router's firewall. Let's see how we can do this.

1 Open up an Internet Explorer window, and type the router IP address in the address bar as before, pressing Enter to visit the setup page

2 Log into the router setup utility using your administrator password

3 Click the Firewall group link

> Firewall

4 Ensure the radio button is set to Enable, and if not, adjust it to this setting. Click the Apply Changes button

Firewall >

Your Router is equipped with a firewall that will protect your network from a wide array of common hacker attacks including Ping of Death (PoD) and Denial of Service (DoS) attacks. You can turn the firewall function off if needed. Turning off the firewall protection will not leave your network completely vulnerable to hacker attacks, but it is recommended that you turn the firewall on whenever possible.

Firewall Enable / Disable >   ⦿ Enable   ◯ Disable

 Clear Changes   Apply Changes

Preventing access by time

Let's imagine that a father is concerned that his daughter, Alysia, is logging on to the Internet when she gets home from school, and as a consequence is not finishing her homework on time for the next day. Whilst he doesn't want to block her access to the Internet totally, he wants to be sure that she has at least a couple of hours free from distractions.

Alysia uses a notebook to connect to the wireless router, and her father has given it an IP address of 192.168.2.15.

We can use the router firewall to block access for the above IP address between certain times. It is a two-stage process. Let's see how it can be done.

1 In an Internet Explorer window, visit your router's setup page, and log in as before

Hot tip

Using rules to block access works best with static IP addresses. Remember that DHCP allocates addresses to computers, so if a computer picks up a different address from that specified in your rule, it will no longer apply to that PC.

2 For the first stage we need to set up a Schedule Rule. Click Client IP Filters, followed by the Schedule Rule link.

Firewall > Client IP filters

>> Access Control   >> URL Blocking   >> Schedule Rule

3 Click Add Schedule Rule

Rule Name	Rule Comment	Configure
	No Valid Schedule Rule !!!	

> Add Schedule Rule

4 Fill in the requested details, giving the rule a name in the Name field, and a description in the Comment field. Note that we've set Alysia to be blocked between 1700 and 1900 in the evening on weekdays, but her weekend access is unaffected

5 Click Apply Changes, and note the new rule

131

Rule Name	Rule Comment	Configure
Block Alysia 1	BlockAlysiaEvenings	Edit Delete

6 Now, we need to move on to specify to the router which notebook Alysia uses, by telling it the fixed IP address. Click the Access Control link, followed by Add PC

Client PC Description	Client PC IP Address	Client Service	Schedule Rule	Configure
		No Valid Filtering Rule !!!		

> **Add PC**

7 Fill in the Client PC Description field with a meaningful description,

Client PC Description > Alysia's Laptop

Client PC IP Address > 15 ~ 15

and enter the IP address range, which in our case will be from 15 to 15, as we only wish to block the IP address for Alysia's notebook, address 15

8 In the table on the same page, tick all of the check boxes, as Alysia's father doesn't want her to use any form of Internet access during the set times

9 Adjust the Scheduling Rule drop-down list to Block Alysia 1, and click Apply Changes

10 Alysia's notebook is now featured in the Client PC list

Client PC Description	Client PC IP Address	Client Service	Schedule Rule	Configure
Alysia's Laptop	192.168.2.15	WWW, WWW with URL Blocking, E-mail Sending, News Forums, E-mail Receiving, HTTPS, FTP, MSN Messenger, Telnet, AIM, NetMeeting, DNS, SNMP, PPTP, L2TP, TCP, UDP	Block Alysia 1	Edit Delete

> **Add PC**

Apply Changes

11 Adjust the Enable Filtering Function radio button to Enable, and click the Apply Changes button

Enable Filtering Function > ⦿ Enable ◯ Disable

12 The rule will now be in force. Log out of the setup utility when you have finished

Control by MAC address

We've taken some major steps in securing our network. If you want control of who can access your network, there is another option which gives you almost total control of access.

The option is MAC address filtering. A MAC address is a unique "number" applied to every network adapter manufactured.

Using the MAC address to control access to your network means that you can specify exactly who can and can't access your network. It takes some extra administrative work, but it is well worth the time spent.

133

1 Firstly, we need to find out the MAC address of the PC we want to grant access to. On that PC, click the Start button, then Control Panel, and double click the Network and Sharing Center icon

2 Click the "Manage network connections" link, and double-click the connection you use to attach to your network

LAN or High-Speed Internet (1)

Local Area Connection
Home Network
SiS 900 PCI Fast Ethernet Ad...

3 Click the Details… button

Details…

4 From the details displayed, carefully make a note of the Physical Address

Description	SiS 900 PCI Fast Ethernet Adapter
Physical Address	00-11-2F-E1-9A-5D
DHCP Enabled	Yes

5 Click Close, and Close again, close the Network Connections window and then exit the Network and Sharing Center

6 We now need to configure the router to allow access to the specified MAC address. Note that the method we are using will only allow PCs with specified MAC addresses access via the router. Therefore, you must take care, and you will need to add the MAC address for every computer you wish to allow access to your network. Log into your router setup utility again through Internet Explorer

Hot tip

MAC stands for Media Access Control.

Hot tip

The term "network adapter" refers to the component in your PC that facilitates a connection to a network.

Beware

Take care when filtering by MAC address. You need to make sure you get the settings right, so that you don't block legitimate computers such as your own.

...cont'd

7 Click the link on the left marked MAC Address Filtering

Client IP Filters
MAC Address Filtering
DMZ

8 Adjust the "Access Rule for registered MAC address" to Allow

Access Rule for registered MAC address > ● Allow ○ Deny

9 Next, enter the relevant MAC address (as obtained in Step 4 earlier and called the "physical address") in the first row of the MAC address table, as below

ID	MAC Address					
1	00	11	2F	E1	9A	5D
2						
3						
4						
5						

10 Finally, adjust the Enable MAC Address Filtering radio button to Enable, and click the Apply Changes button

Firewall > MAC Address Filtering

This feature lets you set up a list of allowed clients. When you enable this feature, you must enter the MAC address of each client on your network to allow network access to each. **More Info**

Enable MAC Address Filtering > ● Enable ○ Disable

If you now try to access your wireless network from any computer without a MAC address entry in your list, it will not connect successfully. Each time somebody wants to connect to your network, you will need to give them access by adding their MAC address to the MAC address filtering list.

MAC address filtering is an excellent method of tightly controlling access to your network, but deserves to be implemented with caution too.

10 Using policies

Just as policies can help businesses and their staff work within common rules and guidelines, setting policies on your PC can ensure users do the same.

136 The Group Policy Editor

137 Getting started

139 Our first policy

143 Securing removable devices

145 Restricting hardware installs

147 Enable administrator access

148 Enable specific device install

The Group Policy Editor

At your place of work, you will almost certainly be working in line with a set of policies, dictated to you by your corporation.

It may be that you feel some policies you work beneath are restrictive and unnecessary. Certainly, many people feel that way.

But what isn't always recognized about policies is that they lend people a framework of protection and structure.

Personal-computer policies

Just as policies are in force in the workplace to protect both the business and the workforce, policies are in place in Windows Vista, to protect the computer and to protect the user too. Similarly to working for a corporation, PC users may feel that they are restricted by the policies in place, but if an element of balance is employed, policies can give enough room for users to be able to do what they need to, whilst providing suitable barriers to protect them, and to protect the PC itself.

A policy example

The good news is that as the administrator of your PC, you have full access to the policies in place and available for use. Policies are an extremely powerful tool, and in terms of security they form a tool that you would not want to leave out of your toolbox.

You may well be thinking that you haven't come across any policies as yet in this book. You may need to think again! Even though it wasn't immediately apparent, we actually adjusted a policy setting back in chapter 3.

Do you recall earlier in the book adjusting an option to enforce password complexity? This was in fact a policy that we were setting, to apply to everyone who would have a user account on the PC. If you chose to set this policy, you should see the policy taking effect every time you change your password.

The Group Policy Editor

So how do we administrate these policies?

The Group Policy Editor is the powerful tool we use to enable and disable policies. The design of the policy editor makes it easy to adjust policies, but exercise some caution when using it.

Let's get started with the Group Policy Editor.

Hot tip

In computing, there is usually more than one way of achieving an objective. The method we used to change the password policy in chapter 3 is different from the method we will be using in this chapter.

Beware

The Policy Editor is a powerful tool and you need to treat it with care and respect. Setting policies can drastically alter the computing experience for you and other users of your PC. Think carefully about any policies you implement.

Getting started

The Group Policy Editor is not included in your Windows Vista menus. Whilst this seems odd for such a powerful tool, it's actually less accessible by design.

As the administrator of your PC, the chances are that you won't want any other users to have access to this tool. Including the tool in the menu structure can inadvertently "advertize" the tool to other users, so it is not launched in that manner.

Launching the Group Policy Editor

We need to launch the Group Policy Editor manually, by running a file. To achieve this we need to temporarily gain access to a "Run" command, so let's set this up first.

Hot tip

The Group Policy Editor is a "snap-in" for a feature known as the "Microsoft Management Console" (MMC). If you decide to become more advanced in administering PCs, you will come across the MMC more often. It allows you to create a customized window with all of your desired "snap-ins" inside, such as the Group Policy Editor and the Event Viewer, to name two examples.

1 Right-click the taskbar, choose Properties, and when the Taskbar and Start Menu Properties window appears, click the Start Menu tab

2 With the radio button set to "Start menu", click the Customize... button

3 Scroll down the list of options until you reach the "Run command" check box. Place a tick in the box

4 Click OK, and then OK again. If you click the Start button, you should now see the Run... button in the bottom right corner, just above the power-switch and padlock buttons

...cont'd

(5) Click the Run... button and in the Open field, type "gpedit.msc"

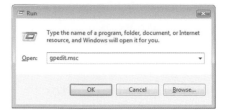

(6) Click OK, and then Continue to the User Account Control warning. The Group Policy Editor will launch

Exploring the Group Policy Editor

Take a moment to explore the Group Policy Editor but take care not to change any settings yet.

You will notice two main sections, Computer Configuration and User Configuration. In the corporate environment, you would be looking to set different policies for different users and groups, which is where the User Configuration section comes into play. The Computer Configuration section deals with policies that affect every user signing on to the PC.

A gentle warning

The Group Policy Editor is a powerful tool, and should be treated with an element of caution. Think about the consequences of any policies you may set, as you need to be careful not to restrict your own access to functions.

So long as you tread steadily with the Group Policy Editor, it will remain a good friend in the battle for PC security.

Beware

It is possible to lock yourself, as an administrator, out of parts of your machine using the Group Policy Editor. Take the greatest of care when using the utility!

Hot tip

Changes made in the Computer Configuration section override changes made in the User Configuration section.

Our first policy

Let's get started on setting a policy. This policy will prevent users of your PC from enabling or disabling add-ons. If you remember add-ons from chapter 7, we learned that not all of the add-ons available are safe to use, and some are even intentionally malicious by design. Taking the ability to enable and disable add-ons from users is a measure you may consider necessary.

Hot tip

Windows Vista has a huge increase in available policies over Windows XP.

1   Launch the Group Policy Editor using the steps described previously

2   In the Computer Configuration section, expand the Administrative Templates group by either double-clicking on it, or clicking the small triangle to the left

Don't forget

As we are changing a policy in the Computer Configuration group, this will apply to all users, including you! Therefore, if you need to enable or disable an add-on, you'll need to disable the policy again.

3   The interface is similar to the Windows Explorer interface, with a left and right pane to navigate through the groups and policies. Now double-click Windows Components and then Internet Explorer

...cont'd

Hot tip

If you want to know what a policy is going to do, click the policy once and a handy description appears to the left of the policy.

4 Double-click the "Do not allow users to enable or disable add-ons" policy

5 Adjust the radio button to Enabled, and click OK. Users are no longer allowed to enable or disable add-ons. Close the Group Policy Editor

Testing our policy
We've set a policy to restrict the management of add-ons, but how can we be sure it's worked? Let's test it.

1 Launch an Internet Explorer session by clicking the Internet Explorer icon

2 Press the Alt key to reveal the menu bar, and click Tools, then Internet Options

Internet Options

3 Click the Programs tab and look at the "Manage add-ons" section. The "Manage add-ons" button is "grayed out" and we can't click it

Manage add-ons

Enable or disable browser add-ons installed in your system.

Manage add-ons

4 Our policy has worked! We can't access the "Manage add-ons" section, and neither can any other users. Click Cancel to return to Internet Explorer

Restricting access to the Group Policy Editor

With earlier versions of Windows, setting policies was a potentially difficult prospect. Due to the fact that many users would be allocated local administrator rights to a PC, a user with a little know-how would be able to simply run the policy editor and undo any changes they didn't want, circumventing the carefully laid policies of the administrator.

Administrators would then try to restrict access to the "gpedit. msc" file, but this could sometimes result in the administrator becoming locked out of the machine too!

The design of Windows Vista makes this prospect far easier. As an administrator, you can allocate administrator rights only when necessary using "over-the-shoulder" credentials, and then the standard user can only use those rights for the specific purpose they have requested. Therefore, once you've set your policies, you need to log off from your administrator account and log back in as a standard user.

Standard users cannot run the Group Policy Editor without you allocating them the rights to do so, so your policies are safe, and won't change unless you choose to change them under your administrator account.

Further locking down Internet Explorer

We successfully removed access for users to enable or disable what could be potentially dangerous add-ons. You can take a stronger line towards preventing browser changes that could introduce security threats by limiting users' access to the Internet Options tabs.

1 Launch the Group Policy Editor once again

Don't forget

Remember to remove the Run command from the Start Menu when you have finished using the Group Policy Editor.

...cont'd

2 Browse to Computer Configuration, Administrative Templates, Windows Components, Internet Explorer, and Internet Control Panel

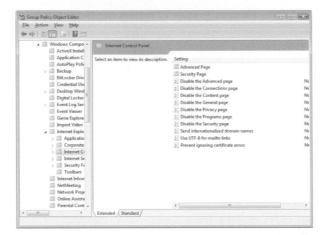

3 Double-click the "Disable the Advanced page" policy, and adjust the radio button to Enabled. Click OK to return to the Group Policy Editor. Repeat this process for all seven pages in the list, and then close the Group Policy Editor

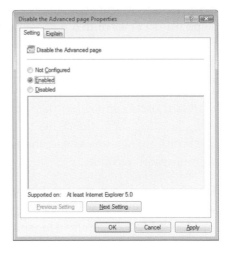

This has restricted access to the Internet Options for all users of your PC. Remember that poor Internet Options choices can lower the security of your browser.

Enabling a disable option

It may strike you as strange that we used "Enabled" on a policy to disable access to an option! The policy states it will "disable the page", so if we enable that policy it actually performs a "disable" on the option, and the page will no longer be accessible.

Hot tip

It may help to remember that two negatives always make a positive. So, if you are "disabling" a "disable" policy, you are enabling the action that the policy applies to.

Securing removable devices

In the early days of PC computing, before networks and email systems were largely established, viruses were spread predominantly by floppy disks. Whilst floppy disks can still pose a threat, their decline in popularity (mainly due to their unreliability and small storage capacity) has meant that virus writers seldom spend their time on exploiting this medium.

The proliferation of USB removable storage devices has meant that viruses are more likely to spread using this form of storage. These devices, with their simple "plug and play" installation process, present a number of threats in today's computing environment:

- The introduction of viruses to your PC

- Infection by spyware, adware, and other malware

- Easier removal of confidential and private information from a PC

From these points, it's clear that you need a strong policy on USB removable storage devices, and the Group Policy Editor helps you to enforce this policy effectively.

1   Launch the Group Policy Editor

2   Expand the Computer Configuration group, and then double-click Administrative Templates, System, Device Installation, and Device Installation Restrictions

Hot tip

USB removable storage devices are sometimes called USB pens or USB keys, as well as USB flash drives.

Beware

If you are using your PC in a business environment, you will need to be extra careful with USB removable storage issues. Implementing an enforced policy through the Group Policy Editor is a good way of ensuring a company removable storage device policy works.

...cont'd

3 Double-click the "Prevent installation of removable devices" policy, and adjust the radio button to Enabled

4 Click OK and then close the Group Policy Editor

Any removable storage device that isn't currently installed will now be prevented from installing, if inserted into the PC.

If a user attempts to install a removable storage device, the driver installation process begins as normal, but a notification message appears:

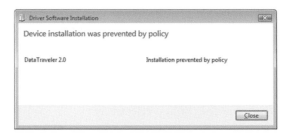

If you check the status of the USB device within Device Manager, it reports that the installation of the device is forbidden by system policy:

Knowing that the removable storage policy has taken effect and is being enforced lends some extra peace of mind.

Hot tip

Using different policies means you can be flexible according to your security needs. If you want to allow users to install USB flash drives but are concerned about confidential data being removed from the machine, enable the "Removable Disks: Deny write access" policy in the Removable Storage Access group. Remember to disable the "Prevent installation of removable devices" policy too.

Restricting hardware installs

Removable storage media such as USB flash drives can present clear threats to the security of your PC and its data. Installing other hardware on your machine can also pose security problems, and it is an element that should be tightly controlled. Allowing others to install hardware may not be a desirable situation.

Let's examine a method of using policies to enforce a framework of control for hardware installations. We'll begin by preventing all hardware installations by policy, and then use the flexibility of the Group Policy Editor to introduce some exceptions to the rule.

1 Launch the Group Policy Editor

2 Expand the Computer Configuration group, and then double-click Administrative Templates, System, Device Installation, and Device Installation Restrictions

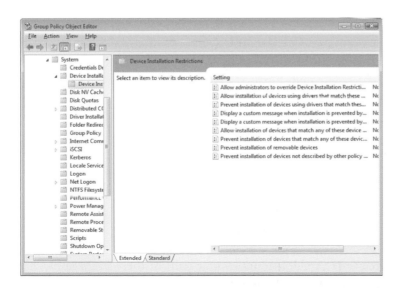

Don't forget

You can find out exactly what a policy does by clicking it once and reading the description to the left. Check what our policy is going to do.

...cont'd

3 Double-click "Prevent installation of devices not described by other policy settings"

4 Adjust the radio button to Enabled and click OK

5 Close the Group Policy Editor

Hot tip

When setting a new policy, consider how it may affect any of your existing policies.

Let's examine what this policy does. It prevents hardware installation of devices "not described by other policy settings". So, the policy is in force, as long as no other policy settings are specifying differently.

But there are a couple of exceptions that it would be handy to make to this rule:

● To have, as the PC administrator, exemption from the hardware installation policy

● To be able to specify certain hardware devices that are authorized to be installed on the system

We can use policies to implement both of these exceptions. Let's look at how over the next two sections.

Enable administrator access

As the administrator of your PC, it isn't a time-efficient option for you to have to adjust a policy every time you want to install some hardware.

Fortunately, we can enable a policy that will give you, as an administrator, the rights to be able to install hardware devices. This policy overrides the "Prevent installation of devices not described by other policy settings" policy that we set earlier.

Don't forget

You should only log in as an administrator to perform specific tasks. Log off as soon as you have finished and use a normal user account for your everyday work.

1 Launch the Group Policy Editor

2 Expand the Computer Configuration group, and then double-click Administrative Templates, System, Device Installation, and Device Installation Restrictions

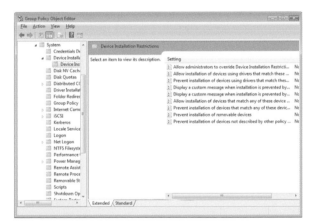

3 Double-click "Allow administrators to override Device Installation Restriction policies"

4 Adjust the radio button to Enabled, and click OK to return to the Group Policy Editor, which you can now close

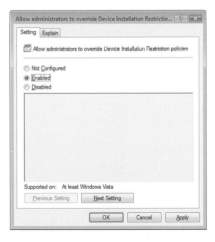

Enable specific device install

Let's review the hardware installation policies we've set so far in this chapter.

- We initially set a policy to prevent removable storage devices, such as USB flash drives, from being installed on our PC

- We then set a policy that prevents all future hardware from being installed on our PC, providing a more complete level of protection

- Since this would prove too restrictive for an administrator, we enabled a policy that overrides these restrictions if you are logged in as an administrator

In terms of hardware installation, our PC is now protected from any hardware that is added without our knowledge. It simply won't install when it is attached, and a policy message will confirm this to the user currently logged in.

We can now use a policy to grant even more control over what hardware can be attached to our machine. Let's imagine that you have allocated a USB flash drive to a user, and you would like to grant this specific device access to the PC. Using the following policy we can begin to build a list of approved devices.

Don't forget

You can still apply policies to restrict read and write access via USB flash drives, which will also apply to our permitted USB flash drive once installed.

1. Launch the Group Policy Editor

2. Expand the Computer Configuration group, and then double-click Administrative Templates, System, Device Installation, and Device Installation Restrictions

3 We need to disable the "Prevent installation of removable devices" policy. This policy will override the policy we are about to set. It is no longer needed, because we still have the "Prevent installation of devices not described by other policy settings" policy enabled, which is protecting our PC from new hardware installations. Double-click the "Prevent installation of removable devices" policy and adjust the radio button to Disabled before clicking OK

Hot tip

If you want to try this policy out on a previously installed USB flash drive, you'll need to remove it from Device Manager first so that the policy will apply to it when it is reinstalled.

4 For the purposes of this example, disable the "Allow administrators to override device installation" policy setting too. If we leave it enabled while logged in as administrator we won't be able to see our new policy taking effect

5 Insert the USB flash drive you wish to feature on our list of approved devices. Vista will begin the installation process, but will present a message to warn that it is being blocked by our policy

...cont'd

6 We now need to tell the policy editor which device we want to grant approval to. We do this by specifying the hardware ID of the device. Click the Start button, followed by Control Panel

7 In Control Panel, double-click the Device Manager icon

Device Manager

8 Click Continue at the User Account Control warning

9 In Device Manager, you should be able to identify your USB device. It will have question-mark and exclamation-mark icons to the left, as our policy will have prevented it from installing

10 Double-click the device and select the Details tab

11 Click "Hardware ids" from the Property drop-down list

12 Right-click the first ID in the list and choose Copy. Exit out of Device Manager and Control Panel

13 Return to the Group Policy Editor, and remaining in the Device Installation Restrictions group, double-click the "Allow installation of devices that match any of these device IDs" policy

(14) Adjust the radio button to Enabled

- ○ Not Configured
- ◉ Enabled
- ○ Disabled

(15) Click the Show… button   [Show...]

(16) Click the Add… button   [Add...]

(17) Right-click and paste the hardware ID information into the field, and click OK

Add Item

Enter the item to be added: [OK]

USBSTOR\DiskKingstonDataTraveler_2.0PMAP   [Cancel]

(18) Click OK, and OK again to return to the Policy Editor

Reinstalling the device

Our USB flash drive is now in the approved-devices list, but it is still restricted by a former policy we set. Let's remove the device from Device Manager and then install it again to see if the new policy permits it.

(1) Click the Start button, followed by Control Panel

(2) Double-click the Device Manager icon once again

(3) Right-click the USB device and select Update Driver Software…

Other devices
DataTraveler 2.0
Multimedia / — Update Driver Software...
Multimedia (— Disable

(4) If you are unaware of the location of drivers for your device, click on "Search automatically for updated driver software"

How do you want to search for driver software?

→ Search automatically for updated driver software
Windows will search your computer and the Internet for the latest driver software for your device.

...cont'd

5 The device should install successfully, and become visible in Device Manager

6 A message should now appear confirming successful installation

7 Click Close to clear the message

8 You can now close Device Manager and Control Panel, and your USB device is ready for use

You should now be able to access any files on the USB flash drive, as it is an approved device. This may have seemed like a long-winded process, but it is well worth the effort to prevent unauthorized people from using USB flash drives to steal your confidential data, whilst not penalizing legitimate USB flash drive users on your PC.

Allowing devices versus denying devices

During the steps in this chapter, you may have noticed the Group Policy Editor also offers the opportunity to explicitly prevent specific removable storage devices from being installed onto your PC, if you specify the hardware ID.

Whilst this may be useful if you know the hardware ID of specific devices that may pose a threat, it is no substitute for blocking all devices and then allowing them on a case-by-case basis. Good security practice involves starting out with universal restrictions, and then carefully opening up areas of safety as required.

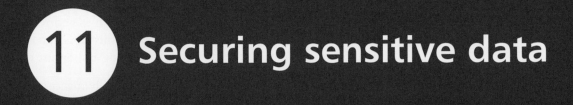

11 Securing sensitive data

You can employ encryption to secure confidential files.

154 What is encryption?

155 Encryption in Vista

156 Other encryption options

What is encryption?

We have seen how you can apply security to your files and folders using the Windows Vista account model, and whilst this can mean a lot of work, it's a solid method of securing important data.

There is another tool to ensure that files are virtually inaccessible to external parties, and it's cropped up in previous chapters.

"Encryption" is an established and powerful method of preventing others from "seeing" the data you have got stored in a file. It effectively "scrambles" the data so that any prying eyes, should they try to look, will see a collection of nonsensical "junk".

You may or may not realize, but encryption is occurring around you all the time. Transactions and purchases made over the Internet are always, or at least should be, encrypted. Companies use encryption to ensure the security of their data and their customers' information, and governments use encryption to disguise confidential and sensitive information.

How does encryption work?

Whilst the mechanics of encrypting a file and its data can be complex, the basic concept of encryption is straightforward.

In order to encrypt the contents of a file, a cipher is required. A cipher is basically an "algorithm", a specified procedure that dictates how the file will be "scrambled". In basic encryption, this can then be used to "decrypt" the file again.

To understand the relationship between encryption and the cipher, try to imagine it as follows:

● You take a pile of highly confidential papers (your data)

● You place them into a room (the file)

● You take a complex door key (the cipher)

● You lock the door with the contents inside, and you notice that when you turn the key some frosted glass appears in the door. If intruders try to look through the thick frosted glass, the glass distorts the contents of anything in the room so that it is completely illegible (encryption)

Nobody can access the room with your information inside without your key, or "cipher".

Encryption in Vista

The Vista file system offers encryption functionality. You may wish to consider using it on confidential and sensitive files. You can choose to encrypt a file, or folder, including its contents.

Encrypting a file

When you encrypt a file, you are also offered the option of encrypting the folder it is stored in. If you prefer, you can encrypt a folder directly by right-clicking the folder instead of a file.

Beware

Encryption is particularly important for notebook users, whose physical hardware is more vulnerable to theft.

1   Launch Windows Explorer, and navigate to the file you wish to encrypt

Hot tip

With Vista, you don't need to be actively involved in applying a cipher to a file for encryption. This is all handled in the "background".

2   Right-click the file and select Properties

3   Click the Advanced button

4   Place a tick in the "Encrypt contents to secure data" check box

5   Click OK, and then OK again. A message appears

6   Adjust the radio button to "Encrypt the file only", if you just wish to encrypt the file itself. If you wish to encrypt the folder it is located in, ensure the radio button is on "Encrypt the file and its parent folder", and click OK

The file is now encrypted. One point to note is that the encryption key is integrated with your user profile, so you need to ensure nobody has any access to your user profile. Never share your password, and log off before you leave your desk.

Beware

When you encrypt a file or folder, notice that a pop-up window occurs asking if you wish to back up your encryption key. This is a vital requirement for important data, because if you lose the encryption key, you won't be able to access the data either!

Other encryption options

Don't forget

Windows Mail offers encryption for sending confidential messages to trusted recipients, as we mentioned in chapter 8.

Hot tip

A famous example of public-key encryption software is Pretty Good Privacy, or PGP, available from www.pgp.com.

Hot tip

If you wish to send encrypted files to others, use the same method. You will need to obtain the recipient's public key to encrypt the file with before sending.

Many of your applications will include encryption options, and getting to know the features of your software is time well spent.

Another option for file security is to use a third-party encryption tool. These are particularly handy for people sending confidential documents across networks or the Internet.

Using encryption for this purpose needs the use of a more advanced form of encryption. The encryption we used for our confidential file in the last example was straightforward. When we encrypted the file, Windows generated an encryption key that is integrated with our user profile. Therefore as long as we are logged in under our own user profile, Windows will automatically use our encryption key to decrypt the files we have encrypted, if we wish to view and work with them.

If we wanted to share a confidential file with another person using this method of encryption, we would need to give them our key, in this case in the form of our user profile. Even giving trusted parties our key and user profile is very bad security practice, so we have to employ an alternative method.

Public-key encryption

Public-key encryption is the accepted answer to this problem. This method involves the use of two keys, a private key and a public key. You need to generate both keys to use this method.

Let's imagine that Richard wants to send you a file but its contents are confidential.

- You make your public key available to Richard (and anyone else whom you wish to receive encrypted files from)

- Richard uses your public key to encrypt the file and sends it to you

- You use your private key, which you are the only person with access to, to decrypt the file Richard has sent to you, and you can then read the contents

The important thing to understand here is that the public key can encrypt the data being sent to you, but only your private key can decrypt it. Therefore, nobody but you can see what is in the file, and nobody has needed to share your private key.

12 Securing Vista

Windows Vista is a very

secure operating system, but

there are some extra security

settings to be aware of.

158   Additional Vista security

159   Disabling services

160   Remote Desktop

161   Windows Explorer

162   File attributes

Additional Vista security

As we've discussed, Vista has been designed by Microsoft with a rigorous regard for security from the ground upwards.

Windows Vista defaults are set to protect you from the numerous security threats that exist in today's interconnected computing environment. Out of the box, Vista is very secure.

Yet there are some elements of Vista security that we need to be aware of for certain circumstances. For instance, if you click to allow a software package to pass by Vista's security measures, and it later turns out to exhibit malicious actions, you may need to understand how you can stop a specific service from running.

We also need to look at some features that users often enable, that should remain disabled.

The Vista Security Center

Windows Vista includes a new feature called the Security Center, which allows you to view and work with the main security elements on your PC all in one place.

1 Click Start, and then Control Panel

2 In Control Panel, double-click the Security Center icon

3 The Security Center warns you if items are out of date. In our example, we are alerted that virus protection and antispyware protection both need updating

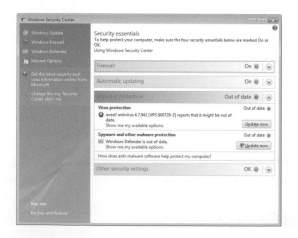

158

Disabling services

As we've mentioned, Windows Vista is secure out of the box. However, some virus, spyware or other malware infections install and start services on your PC. On occasion, antivirus companies supply removal procedures that require you to stop services.

Services are programs that run in the "background" of Windows. You don't notice them in the same sense as standard applications, such as your word processor or spreadsheet, but they are often fulfilling essential "behind the scenes" duties.

Controlling services

Let's look at how we can control services running on Vista.

1 Click Start, and then Control Panel

2 Double-click the Administrative Tools icon

Administrativ
e Tools

3 Double-click the Services shortcut

Reliability and Performance Monitor	11/2/2006 12:52 PM	Shortcut	2 KB
Services	11/2/2006 12:52 PM	Shortcut	2 KB
System Configuration	11/2/2006 12:51 PM	Shortcut	2 KB

4 Click Continue at the User Account Control warning, and have a look at the list of services running on our PC

5 Scroll down the list and, for the sake of this example, double-click the Offline Files service. Notice that this service has a state of "Started". This means it is running in the background at the moment

6 If you believe a service to be causing a problem or to be malicious in any way, you need to click the Stop button immediately

Service status: Started

Start | Stop | Pause | Resume

7 To prevent a service from running at startup, click the "Startup type" drop-down list and select Disabled

Startup type: Automatic
                Automatic (Delayed Start)
Help me configure Automatic
                Manual
                Disabled
Service status: Started

Remote Desktop

Beware

If Remote Desktop is enabled, then users with administrator rights for the PC can connect across remotely and use the machine, even if they are not members of the Remote Desktop group. This is another good reason to limit the administrator account to one.

Remote Desktop is a useful feature that has transformed the potential for remotely supporting Windows PCs. It allows a user at another computer to log onto your PC for support purposes.

Whilst this is a handy feature, it is recommended that you only enable it when strictly required and disable it straight afterwards.

By default Remote Desktop is disabled in Windows Vista, but let's see where we control Remote Desktop access, in case the PC you are administering has had this default adjusted.

1 Click the Start button and then Control Panel

2 Double-click the System icon

3 Click the Remote Settings link at the left side, and click Continue past the User Account Control warning to move to the Remote System Properties window

4 Ensure that the Remote Desktop options radio button is set to "Don't allow connections to this computer", and also ensure that the "Allow Remote Assistance connections to this computer" check box is unchecked, too

5 Click the Select Users… button and remove anyone you feel should not have remote access to your PC. You can always re-add people at a later stage

Windows Explorer

With modern users likely to use a variety of file formats, such as music files, movies, documents, spreadsheets, and digital images, it is inevitable that they will perform more processes with files stored on the PC.

As a consequence, you need to make sure that your PC is set up to minimize the potential for mistakes, and to ensure the security of your essential system files.

We need to review some options in Windows Explorer, the part of Windows that enables people to perform file movements and maintenance, and ensure that the most secure options are in place.

1 Launch Windows Explorer by clicking the Start button, followed by All Programs, Accessories, and Windows Explorer

2 When Explorer has launched, press the Alt key once to reveal the menu bar, and click Tools

Hot tip

You can set a policy to hide the Folder Options menu option. This means that users have no access to adjust these settings and consequently can't "undo" the security you have implemented here. Use the skills you learned in chapter 10 to enable a policy in User Configuration, Administrative Templates, Windows Components, Windows Explorer. The policy is called "Removes the Folder Options menu item from the Tools menu".

3 Click Folder Options, followed by the View tab

4 Scroll down and ensure that the following options have been set. The radio button for "Do not show hidden files and folders" ensures that any files with a "hidden" attribute remain hidden from users, and the ticked check box for "Hide protected operating system files" also obscures the critical Windows system files from users. The other ticked check box hides known file extensions, such as .exe and .doc, from users, which helps to prevent file extensions from being accidentally renamed.

File attributes

Implementing secure and comprehensive file security across your PC is a task that necessitates a lot of careful thought and consideration. We covered security for users in chapter 5 and this should have given you the foundation of skills to begin constructing a solid and secure framework of file security for your users.

Whilst securing files on your PC in this manner is an irreplaceable option, there are some occasions when you may wish to adjust attributes for specific files. Let's look at the two attributes you can set on a file.

Read-only
Enabling the "read-only" file attribute means that the file can be accessed by those in the access list but it cannot be modified by anyone. You may wish to use this option if you have a file that you are happy for users in the access list to open, but you would not like anyone to modify.

Hidden
The "hidden" file attribute will make a file invisible to users when they browse to the folder it is located in. This can be useful if you have to store a file in a specific folder but you would rather others using the folder did not attempt to open or change it. If you wish to view it again, you need to adjust the "Do not show hidden files and folders" option that we checked in the last section.

Adjusting attributes
Let's try changing some attributes on a folder.

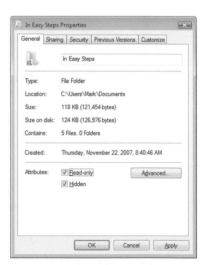

1 Launch Windows Explorer and navigate to the file you wish to adjust

2 Right-click the file and choose Properties

3 Click the Read-only or Hidden attributes as required, and click OK when finished

Beware

Implementing file security across a PC is an important job, but if you are administering multiple PCs across a network your job will be much bigger! Bear this in mind if you attach your PC to a network.

Hot tip

You can apply the same attributes to Windows folders too.

Hot tip

Hidden files are not seen in Windows Explorer if you have set the "Do not show hidden files and folders" option in the Windows Explorer Folder Options, as we looked at in the last section.

13 Securing applications

The applications on your PC

may need securing too.

164 Securing your applications

165 Disabling macros

167 Password-protecting files

Securing your applications

If you've been implementing the measures advised in this book so far, you may now be in a situation where you've got many layers of security in place to protect you.

● You may now be more security-savvy yourself, and you've hopefully enjoyed some level of success passing the important elements of what you've learned to other users of your PC

● You may be sitting behind the trusty security of a hardware and software firewall, a reassuring combination indeed

● Your antispyware software is active and protecting you against all sorts of malicious programs, and your antivirus software should be up to date and warding off any chance of infection

● There should be multiple other functions protecting you as well, ranging from the tight control of system policies, through to the benefits of the User Account Control function

So what else could we possibly need to worry about? Well, let's imagine that you choose to install an application onto your machine, whether this is a music playback application, a new graphics package, or an accounting tool. When you install the new program, Windows User Account Control will warn you and ask if you want to proceed, which you will agree to. If it communicates over the Internet, you may be happy to allow it to be unblocked by the firewall.

The problem is, after all the layers of security you've painstakingly built up, you can inadvertently reintroduce security threats by allowing installed applications to circumvent your security measures!

Know your application

Today's applications are complex, and you can't hope to know and understand every element within a package. But a little reading and research into applications can pay dividends. Whilst using a package, consider these points:

● If it requests firewall access, why does it need it?

● Are there any reports on the application's website concerning security issues?

● Are there any reports on the web of security issues?

Hot tip

Applications rarely arrive with paper manuals today, so getting to know your application may mean browsing an online manual, or one on a supplied CD. This can be handy, as you can run searches for specific information, such as "security".

Disabling macros

Let's look at a couple of examples of application security. We're going to use the Microsoft Office 2007 suite as the example package. This isn't because Microsoft Office is a particular threat to your system's security, but rather that this information should be applicable to a wider range of users.

Let's investigate how we can manage macros in Microsoft Office 2007.

What is a macro?

Macros are a handy function within many applications, and the Microsoft Office 2007 suite offers the use of macros in its component parts, such as Word, and Excel.

Macros can be used to automate repetitive tasks, from very basic functions such as inserting some formatted text in a Word document, to advanced complex calculations.

Macros become a security vulnerability because they are so powerful. Whilst it is possible to "record and playback" a sequence of events for a macro, you can also use a programming language. Malicious programmers have abused the power of macros to write viruses and other malware, so you need to be on your guard.

Ensuring safety from dangerous macros

Microsoft Office 2007 is protected against macros by default, but it's worth us taking a look at the settings for a number of reasons:

- Somebody may have changed the macro security level

- We can introduce the important concept of the Trust Center

- We can see how application security is important, too

Open Microsoft Excel, and run through the following steps.

 Click the Microsoft Office button

2 Click the Excel Options button at the foot of the box

Hot tip

With the default Microsoft Office 2007 settings, macros are dealt with securely.

Beware

Microsoft Word has been exploited in the past to create macro viruses.

Beware

Macro viruses are likely to arrive as attachments, so be discriminating as to which attachments you open. If in doubt, delete the message.

165

...cont'd

③ Click the Trust Center button

> `Trust Center`

④ Click the Trust Center Settings... button

> `Trust Center Settings...`

⑤ Click to select the Macro Settings group in orange and take a look at the available options

> **Macro Settings**
>
> For macros in documents not in a trusted location:
> ○ Disable all macros without notification
> ◉ Disable all macros with notification
> ○ Disable all macros except digitally signed macros
> ○ Enable all macros (not recommended; potentially dangerous code can run)

Beware

Even if you receive many files containing macros, don't be tempted to choose the "Enable all macros" option for the sake of convenience.

166

⑥ Selecting the "Enable all macros" radio button would be a bad move. This would allow any macro, dangerous or otherwise, to run on your machine. If it is not set to the "Disable all macros with notification" option, then change it to this now by clicking the radio button

> ◉ **Disable all macros with notification**

⑦ Click OK, then OK again to return to Microsoft Excel

A note about the Trust Center

Microsoft Office 2007 includes a new facility where you can adjust privacy and security settings across the entire Office suite. Therefore, when you set security levels on, say, macros, these levels apply across the whole suite of products, including Word, Excel, Access, and Powerpoint.

Powerful features such as the Trust Center reflect Microsoft's increased focus on making security more powerful, whilst becoming easier to implement across related products. The result should be tighter security and a reduction in administration of security.

Don't forget

Being able to adjust security across related products makes good sense, but always be aware that any lowering of security also affects the related products.

Password-protecting files

The User Account model utilized by Windows Vista means that users have greater file security. By its very design, Vista lends better protection to people's documents.

However, let's consider the following situations:

- You want to place a document into the Public folder, and people to read it, but you don't want people to modify it

- You want to share a document with a trusted user but nobody else

- You have a very important and confidential document that you want to be sure nobody else can access

- You would like to email a confidential document to another person but are concerned about it being intercepted or accessed by an unauthorized user

Whilst sharing the file on your own PC, you can of course apply security to the file as we saw in chapter 5, "Security for users". But if you are sending the file across the email system to another user, then your local PC security won't apply in the same way. So the best solution is to apply a password to the document and share this with your trusted user.

Password-protecting a Microsoft Word document

Let's examine how we can password-protect a file in Microsoft Word.

1   Create a new Word document, or open a document you wish to protect with a password

2   Click the Microsoft Office button

3   Click the Save As button to open the Save As window

Don't forget

Be sure to follow the rules for strong passwords as detailed in chapter 3. Encourage other users of the PC to follow these rules too.

Beware

If you are sending a password-protected document to another person, be sure not to use a password you use for other purposes, as this creates a security vulnerability, no matter how much you trust the recipient.

Hot tip

Similar password-protect options are available in other Microsoft Office suite applications.

...cont'd

4 Click on the Tools button

5 Select General Options...

6 The General Options window opens

7 Notice that there are two password options in the General Options window. Using the "Password to open" option means that people will not be able to open the file at all without entering the password. Using the "Password to modify" option means that users can open the document but need to enter the password to make any changes to the document. Enter a password in the appropriate field, and click OK

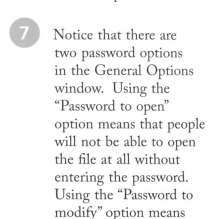

8 Enter the password to confirm, click OK again, and then enter a name to save the file as normal. The password protection is now in effect on the document

Combinations

You can take advantage of the two password options and combine them to implement more advanced password protection. Let's imagine that you have created a confidential document, and would like to distribute it to a group of ten people. However, you would only like a select five of these people to be able to actually modify the document. You could set a password for opening the document, and a different password for modifying the document. You would then need to distribute the document and the password to open the document to all ten users. Then, you would separately supply the modify password to your chosen five users.

14 Using resources

We can't anticipate all security issues, so you need access to security resources

170 Security resources

171 The Microsoft website

173 Microsoft TechNet

174 Newsgroups

Security resources

Since the personal computer was first developed and marketed, the desire to share information between computers has resulted in an explosive growth of computer networking technology, and the world's largest network, the Internet, continues its growth unabated.

As we've seen in this book, this continual progress has seen the introduction of numerous threats that exploit any holes or opportunities available to spread their menace amongst unsuspecting computer users.

It's therefore very satisfying to see that the negative elements of modern computing are countered by a warm and positive user community of professionals, enthusiasts, and everyday users, who eagerly share their security information to help each other stay safe.

Knowing where to look

It's more than a little ironic that the best place to look for information on the security threats that often come from the Internet is, of course, the Internet. The best sources of security information online include:

- Web pages
- Email updates and newsletters
- Message boards
- Microsoft TechNet

Getting the right information

Fortunately, most of the information posted on the web regarding PC security is written in good faith and is largely accurate. Be discriminating though, and use the more established sites for important security advice.

When you discover useful security resources on the web, remember to add them to your favorites list. You can do this by pressing the Ctrl and D keys while on the web page, or by clicking the button with a green cross and yellow star toward the top left of the window, as shown.

Hot tip

The accumulation of PC security information for all users is only really effective if as many people as possible contribute. Even if you have resolved a security issue, try to share this information with others.

170

Beware

Build up a collection of websites whose security advice you trust. Remember that some websites purport to be supplying antispyware software but are in fact trying to encourage you to install spyware or other malware!

The Microsoft website

As you might expect, one of the first places to visit for security information is the Microsoft website, at www.microsoft.com.

The Microsoft website is crammed full of useful security information, guidelines, and advice. Furthermore, it holds a huge knowledge base of known problems.

Getting started on the Microsoft website

Let's have a brief look at some of the areas regarding PC security.

Hot tip

Information is being updated and added to the Microsoft website all the time. Check back regularly for the latest news and alerts.

1 Open up Internet Explorer and in the address bar, type "www.microsoft.com/security", hitting Enter to visit the site

2 Take a minute to explore the site. It's worth glancing at the top stories as these will be pertinent to current security issues

3 There are different sections of the security page defined by role. There are sections for consumers, IT professionals, developers and businesses. Click the Consumers link

Consumers

...cont'd

4 In the list of resources offered to consumers, there is a link to sign up for the consumer security newsletter. Click this link

Stay informed
• Sign-up for the consumer security newsletter

5 Click the "Sign up" link and enter your details to receive the Microsoft Security for Home Computer Users Newsletter

Get the Microsoft Security for Home Computer Users Newsletter

Sign up for our free, monthly e-mail newsletter that's packed with valuable information to help you protect your h computer. This newsletter provides practical security tips for you and your family, useful resources and links, and for you to provide feedback and ask security-related questions.

The Microsoft Knowledge Base

The Microsoft Knowledge Base is a detailed and comprehensive collection of documents covering a huge range of troubleshooting information and other important articles. Many of these cover security issues. Let's take a quick look at the knowledge base.

1 Launch Internet Explorer, and in the address bar enter "support.microsoft.com/search"

2 Select the product you wish to search on from the drop-down list, and enter any relevant search words in the For field. Click Search to find the results. Click on a result to see the corresponding knowledge base article

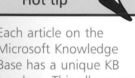

Microsoft TechNet

TechNet is a long-established Microsoft service that provides technical information across a wide range of its products. Whilst subscribers gain access to extra resources and breaking information, you can still take advantage of a huge collection of material for free.

Hot tip

If you work in an IT capacity, signing up to TechNet could pay dividends in the long term, with monthly deliveries of the latest information on CD or DVD.

1 Launch a new Internet Explorer window, or open a new tab if you still have a window open

2 Type "www.microsoft.com/technet" in the address bar and press Enter

3 Let's learn about Vista security features. Click the Windows Vista link at the left menu bar

Windows Vista

4 Click the Security and Protection link

Security and Protection
Discover how to help protect your system and data from malicious attacks with tools, practice labs, and related articles.

5 Scroll down the list and click on the "Windows Vista security guide" link

Windows Vista security guide

6 Browse the information to learn more about Windows Vista security

Newsgroups

The PC community tends to be a positive and supportive group of users. Newsgroups date back to the roots of this community and you can still find some useful information on security issues today.

Let's briefly set up access to newsgroups, and then have a look at a PC security newsgroup.

Before we start, you'll need the following details from your Internet service provider, which you should find on their website:

- Your newsgroup ID

- Your newsgroup password

- The news server name

1 Launch Windows Mail, and click Tools on the menu bar, followed by Accounts…

Newsgroups...	Ctrl+W
Accounts...	
Junk E-mail Options...	

2 Click the Add… button

Add...

3 The Select Account Type window appears. Select Newsgroup Account and click Next

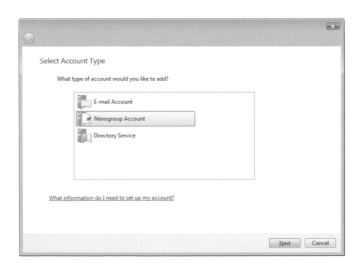

174

4 Enter your name in the "Display name" field and click Next

> When you post a message to a newsgroup or send an e-mail message, your display name will appear in the From field. Type your name as you would like it to appear.
>
> Display name: `Mark Lee`
>
> For example: John Smith

5 Enter your email address in the "E-mail address" field and click Next

> People can reply to your news messages by sending you an e-mail message at the address below--or they may post another news message.
>
> E-mail address: `mark@mail.com`
>
> For example: someone@microsoft.com

6 Enter the name of the news server, as provided by your ISP, and click Next

> Type the name of the Internet news (NNTP) server your Internet service provider has given you.
>
> News (NNTP) server:
>
> `news.news.com`
>
> If your Internet service provider has informed you that you must log on to your news (NNTP) server and has provided you with an NNTP account name and password, then select the check box below.
>
> ☐ My news server requires me to log on

7 Click Finish, and then Close   `Finish`

8 Windows Mail will ask if you want to download newsgroups. Click Yes, and Windows Mail will build a list of available newsgroups

> Windows Mail
>
> ⓘ You are not subscribed to any newsgroups in this account. Would you like to view a list of available newsgroups now?
>
> [Yes] [No]
>
> Get help from communities

9 To subscribe to a newsgroup, simply click to highlight it, and click Subscribe. The newsgroup will appear in the folder list at the left of the Windows Mail window, below your news server name. In the example below I've subscribed to one of the Microsoft Help Groups

> ▲ 📁 Microsoft Communities
>   📄 **microsoft.public.windows.vista.security** (3586)
> 📁 news.freenetname.co.uk

Hot tip

The name you enter in the "Display name" field will be the name that appears on your newsgroup posts.

Beware

You may want to use a temporary email address for newsgroup postings, as spammers try to harvest email addresses from sources such as these.

Hot tip

If your ISP provided you with a separate logon name and password for the news server, you need to tick the "My news server requires me to log on" box and enter the details accordingly.

...cont'd

Don't forget

It is in the community spirit to help others in newsgroups, if you can, as well as asking for help yourself.

Don't forget

While using newsgroups, it is good etiquette to avoid drifting "off topic", and to start a new topic if you wish to raise a separate subject.

Once you've subscribed to a newsgroup, you are free to participate in any subjects that have been posted, or to post your own subjects.

Here's a quick guide to newsgroup postings.

1 Double-click a posting to read it

2 Click the paper-and-pen icon button in the top left of Windows Mail to create a new post. Ensure you have the relevant newsgroup selected

3 If you wish to reply to a posting but only to the person who started the post, open the post and click Reply

4 If you wish to reply to the whole newsgroup, click the Reply Group button

5 Always be polite and positive, and remember to share your knowledge and experiences, too

Message boards and forums

Another option for discussing and researching security issues is the use of online message boards and forums. Similar to newsgroups, message boards and forums are located at websites for people to be able to discuss various issues.

Often, you will need to log in to actually make new posts or reply to existing posts. The good news is that most websites of this type allow you to read and browse through the existing messages without logging in.

For reading about security issues and obtaining practical advice on specific errors or problems, message boards and forums are a real treasure trove of information.

The same rules apply as for newsgroups. Be polite, be positive, and help other people as they will be willing to help you.

15 Disposing of your PC

PC security issues persist

after the lifetime of your PC.

We need to dispose with care.

178 Retiring your PC

179 Preparing to format

180 Formatting the drive

182 Destroying your drive

Retiring your PC

With the rapid developments in computing technology today, it seems like no time at all after you've purchased your powerful new PC that you are making it redundant in favour of a newer, faster, and more functional model.

So, what should you do with a redundant PC? Many people pass them on to others, sell them, give them to charity, or hand them over to a disposal or recycling center.

The problem is that passing your PC on to another party without taking suitable measures poses a very real security threat. Even if you think you have deleted all of your files, there could be a possibility of a malicious individual recovering some or all of your "deleted" information and exploiting it accordingly.

What information was stored on your PC?

When retiring your PC and considering the steps you are taking to dispose of it, try to remember all of the types of information you stored or accessed on the PC. Then consider the consequences of allowing a malicious individual the opportunity of recovering this information.

Decommissioning measures

It's useful to see the redundancy of your PC as a "decommissioning" process. There are a number of measures you need to take when putting your PC out to pasture, and if you follow the steps in this chapter your important data will be inaccessible and unrecoverable.

Let's briefly run through the steps you need to take to make sure that your data is completely destroyed when retiring your PC.

- Manually delete all of your documents, history, images, and any other stored files

- Format your hard drive using Windows

- Format your hard drive using a specific formatting utility

- Physically destroy the hard drive, or use a degaussing tool, or both.

- Dispose of the drive

Let's look at these steps in more detail over the next sections.

Don't forget

The PC you are retiring may hold some of the most important information you own, and even if you think you have deleted everything, traces may remain.

Beware

In contrast to security threats that occur on a live and active PC, you have little chance of discovering if your retired PC has data stolen from it. Once it is out of your sight, you need to be certain that no traces of data are left.

Beware

Deleting your files from a hard drive is not enough to guarantee that the data is inaccessible and unrecoverable. Formatting the drive does not always remove the possibility of data recovery either. Make sure you follow the advised steps carefully and thoroughly.

Preparing to format

Formatting the hard drive inside your redundant PC is the first step toward minimizing the possibility that anyone will be able to steal the information stored on the hard drive after you have disposed of it.

What is formatting?

Formatting a hard drive invokes a process that prepares a disk for use with an operating system. It's possible you may have performed formats on floppy disks, or hard drives.

The result of a format process is that the disk is ready to be accessed by an operating system, and also that it is blank.

However, you need to bear in mind that although the disk may be blank in the eyes of the operating system, the data is usually still on the disk, and using the right tools it will be accessible. Even so, formatting a disk is the first step we need to take in putting our old data out of reach of malicious individuals.

Prior to the format

Before you finally format your redundant hard disk, consider the following points:

- Have you backed up any important information you wish to keep or transfer to your new PC?

- Have you cleared any browsing history in Internet Explorer or your chosen web browser?

- Have all other users of the old PC confirmed that they don't require any further files from the machine?

Formatting a hard disk

There are a few methods you can use to format the old hard disk:

- Boot up the PC with a Windows operating system CD in the drive, commence the installation process, and instruct the setup process to format the drive

- Boot up the PC with a Microsoft DOS "boot" disk, use the "fdisk" tool to delete the hard-disk partitions and replace them with new partitions, and then format the partitioned space

- Insert the hard disk into another PC as a secondary drive and use Windows Vista to format the drive

Don't forget

Computer components, including hard disks, are being replaced at a faster rate than ever, and as a result there is a huge volume of computer waste in the world. Consider the environment when disposing of your PC, and once your data is destroyed ensure you either donate your PC or arrange to have it recycled responsibly.

179

Hot tip

Some people recommend distributing separate pieces of the remains of a destroyed hard disk to different disposal locations at different times for an extremely secure mode of disposal.

Formatting the drive

Whilst all three options are adequate to perform a format of the hard disk, our favored option is the third one, to utilize Windows Vista to perform the format.

To achieve this, you need to remove the hard disk from the old PC, and then install it as a secondary disk in a PC running Vista. Whilst this doesn't require a huge amount of work, we would need space beyond the scope of this chapter to outline the steps required. If you are unsure of what to do, see if a friend or IT colleague will help you with the process.

Formatting a secondary drive with Windows Vista

OK, let's start from the point where you have installed your old hard disk into a PC running Windows Vista. We'll assume, for the purposes of these steps, that there are three hard disks in the PC, the main hard disk running Windows Vista, a secondary drive, and the drive from the old PC.

1 Once the drive is in place, power up the PC and log in

2 Click the Start button, and then Control Panel

3 Double-click the Administrative Tools icon

4 Double-click the Computer Management tool

5 Click Continue at the User Account Control warning, and the Computer Management window will launch

6 Click Disk Management in the Storage group

7 Take a minute to examine the disk-management screen, and carefully identify the disk you want to format. In our example the disk has been installed as a second disk in the machine, labelled "Disk 2". Be careful not to confuse the disk we wish to format with "removable" disks, which may take other drive letters. Check that the drive name and size details are accurate

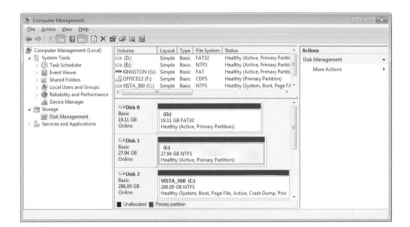

8 Right-click the drive and choose Format...

9 If you are certain that you have selected the correct drive, click Yes to the warning message

Note that the format could take a long time to run. Don't reboot the PC during this time.

Beware

If you have multiple hard drives in your computer already, take the greatest of care to pick the correct one when formatting. Although Windows won't let you format the drive it is running the operating system from, it will let you format your other drives. Remember that data-recovery services are expensive!

Beware

Multiple studies have suggested that from random samples of discarded PCs and their hard drives, almost half of those examined contain data of a confidential nature. The data discovered could often be used for identity theft, fraud, and even as material for blackmail. Make sure that your redundant PC is not part of this statistic!

Hot tip

Once formatted, you may wish to leave the secondary drive in your PC and use it as some extra storage space.

Destroying your drive

It seems extreme, but most experts agree that the only method of putting your hard disk beyond recovery is to physically destroy it.

Some people dismantle the hard disk, pull the internal disk platters apart, and dispose of them accordingly. Paying to have the platters shredded then renders the data truly unrecoverable.

Others argue that the best way to destroy data on a hard drive is by using extremes of heat on the disk platter surfaces.

Some opt to carry out these methods themselves, but dismantling the hermetically-sealed hard drive and then using aggressive means to destroy it are not recommended. It is advisable that once you have performed all of your data-wiping measures on the drive you pass it to a specialist company that will destroy the drive securely for you. Ensure that you select an established and trusted company.

Degaussing your old hard drive

If you have access to a degaussing machine, perhaps at your workplace, or at a local computer services company, it's a good move to carry out a degaussing process on your drive before it is physically destroyed.

If you take the steps of deleting your data, formatting the drive, overwriting it with zeros and ones using specialist software, degaussing the drive, and then having it physically destroyed with heat or shredding, then your data will be as close to unrecoverable as it is possible to get!

The degausser below is from the www.veritysystems.com website:

Don't forget

You may also have data stored on redundant floppy disks, USB flash drives, external hard drives, CD-Rs, CD-RWs, DVDs, and other removable storage. Remember to delete the data on these too, where it is still accessible, and arrange to have the physical hardware destroyed securely.

Hot tip

Businesses in particular would benefit from the services of a data disposal company, where disks may contain confidential business and customer data, and where the turnover of redundant drives may be high.

Beware

If the hard drive on your active PC develops a failure and you can't access your files anymore, you still need to take the same disposal measures outlined in this chapter. Just because you have "lost" your data doesn't mean others can't recover it!

16 Staying protected

You need to stay on top of

changes in PC security.

184   Computing today

185   Windows Update

186   Using Event Viewer

Computing today

Throughout this book, we've seen the ways in which personal computing has changed through the last couple of decades, and the risks that these changes have introduced. Some of the wide spectrum of risks that have emerged over the years include:

- Online identity theft, via hacking or phishing efforts

- Viruses, trojan horses, and worms, and their associated payloads

- Spyware, adware, and other malware

- Junk email, or "spam"

- Direct denial of service attacks

- Attempts to turn your computer into a "zombie" PC (which are often responsible for spam distribution or direct denial of service attacks)

- Rootkits

- Remote hackers trying to access your PC and its valuable data

The world of computing for today's user is very different from that of the PC user five, ten, fifteen, or twenty years ago. From the rapid development of computer-related risks, many of which have taken advantage of the evolution of networking and the Internet, it is clear to see that the sphere of computer security is ever-developing.

By the same token, as a computer user, you need to keep up with the security measures required to provide continual protection of your PC and its data. Whilst the measures in this book help to protect you against the threats in the field today, you need to continually update your knowledge to counter the threats emerging in tomorrow's world.

Whilst it's impossible to future-proof your PC, let's look at some of the ways you can provide ongoing protection as malicious threats develop.

Hot tip

A collection of zombie computers distributing spam or executing direct denial of service attacks is known as a "botnet".

184

Don't forget

Take advantage of online documents, message boards, forums, news articles, and security websites to keep on top of changes in PC security requirements, threats, and vulnerabilities.

Windows Update

Microsoft is aware of the perpetually changing nature of PC security, and as a response it provides mechanisms to ensure that your installation is protected against new potential risks.

One of the most vital mechanisms in achieving this is Windows Update. To understand how Windows Update works, you first need to understand some important concepts about how Microsoft deals with new risks and discovered vulnerabilities.

Patches

When vulnerabilities, security holes, and bugs are discovered in Windows, Microsoft develop a "patch" for users to download and install. The patch contains fresh computer programming code which covers the security hole and protects the computer against the discovered vulnerabilities.

Service Packs

Service Packs are collections of patches, updates, and fixes installed in one tidy package, and can sometimes be a safer way of installing multiple patches, as opposed to installing them individually. These sometimes bring new features to the operating system too.

Using Windows Update

The good news is that Windows Update can do the hard work for you. By default, Windows Update is enabled. Let's check that it is protecting your computer automatically:

1. Click the Start button, then Control Panel

2. Double-click the Windows Update icon

Windows Update

3. Windows should report that it is up to date. Click the "Change settings" link

4. Adjust the radio button to "Install updates automatically", if it is not already selected, and then click OK. You are now protected automatically by Windows Update

Hot tip

Facilities such as Windows Update are sometimes referred to as "patch management" utilities.

185

Hot tip

Allowing Windows Update to automatically protect your PC is the best way to ensure you have the latest patches, fixes, and Service Packs installed. However, if you are using your PC for a critical or mission-critical purpose, you may wish to choose "Download updates but let me choose whether to install them", so that you can vet the patch for any effects it may have on your software or configuration first.

Using Event Viewer

Protection measures such as antivirus software, antispyware software, and your firewall have mechanisms for informing you of any alerts, intrusions, or breaches of security. You should regularly check the log files that these protective measures create, and stay on top of what is going on "behind the scenes" on your PC.

Another area you should check regularly is the Event Viewer. Vista records all notable events occurring on your PC and notes the details into event logs. Let's see how we examine event logs.

1 Click the Start button, and then Control Panel

2 Double-click the Administrative Tools icon

3 In the Administrative Tools list, double-click Event Viewer, and click Continue at the User Account Control warning

4 The Event Viewer window will launch

5 Notice the summary of recently recorded events. To select a particular log, look inside the folders on the left. For instance, if you wish to see the security logs, expand the "Windows Logs" folder, and click on Security

6 Double-click a log item to see details of the particular entry, and click Close, followed by File and Exit when finished

Index

A

Administrative Tools   30, 93–94, 159, 180, 186
Administrator   38–40
  defined   38
  limiting use of   49
  pre-Vista use of local rights   51
  shield icon   51
Administrator Approval Mode   40, 51
Adware   10–11, 66–68, 73–74, 143, 184
Applications
  Microsoft Office 2007   165–166, 168
    Word   61, 165–166, 168
  password-protecting   167
  securing   164

B

Backup media considerations   24
BIOS   32–36
  keystrokes to enter   33
  Phoenix-Award   32, 35
  Supervisor password   34
  User password   34
Botnet   184

C

Certificates   74–75, 78
  certification authority   78
    Comodo   78
    Entrust   78
    Go Daddy   78
    VeriSign   78
  padlock symbol   74
Children
  modern concerns   52

CMOS

CMOS   32, 36
  abbreviation   32
  battery   32, 36
Common sense   79
Community   63, 70, 72, 170, 174, 176

D

Degaussing   178, 182
  degausser machine   182
Destroying a hard disk   182
DHCP   127–128, 131
Dial-up   66
Direct denial of service (DDoS) attacks 12, 57, 67, 184
Disk Management   181
DNS (Domain Name System)   128–129
Downloading 26, 58, 62, 69, 74, 99, 102, 175, 185

E

eBay   12, 103
  Security and Resolution Center   103
Email
  attachments   10, 20–21, 62, 98, 116, 165
  blacklists   109
  filtering   108
  history of security   98
  HTML   102, 117
  mail sending format   117
  security   98
  using plain text   98, 117
Encryption   78, 98, 154–156
  algorithm   154
  basic concept   154
  cipher   154–155
  email   98
  encrypting files and folders   155
  Enigma machine   154

locked-room analogy   154
Pretty Good Privacy (PGP)   156
private key   156
public key   156
Event Viewer   137, 186

limiting access to Internet Options   141
policies   136, 138–148, 164
restricting access to   141
restricting hardware installs   145
securing removable devices   143

F

FDC (Floppy Disk Controller)   35–36
Files
    permissions   45–47
    securing   45
File and Printer Sharing   47, 92, 96, 122
File attributes   162
    adjusting   162
    hidden   162
    read-only   162
File extensions   74, 89, 161
Firewall   68,
    75, 90–94, 108, 123–124, 130–132, 164, 186
    origin of term   90
    wall analogy   90
Floppy disks   9, 22, 57, 62, 143, 179, 182
Floppy drive   22, 35–36
    removing   36
Formatting   117, 125, 128, 178–181
    hard disk   179
        DBAN   180
        using Windows Vista   180
Forums   26, 74, 108, 176, 184

G

Grayware   10
Groups   48–50
Group Policy Editor   136–152, 186
    disable add-ons   140
    enable administrator access   147
    enable specific device install   148
    enabling disable options   142
    example policy   136
    getting started   137
    hide folder options   161
    launching   137

H

Hackers   11–14, 26, 28,
    35, 50, 66–67, 74–75, 89, 93, 127, 168, 184
"cracker" term   12
method of operation   13
    keystroke capture   14
    network tools   13
    social engineering   13
psychology   13, 64
Hexadecimal   125

I

Identity fraud   19, 57, 76, 98
Identity theft   8, 19, 181
Instant messaging   62
Internet   9, 11, 13, 15, 22, 26, 52, 57–58,
    62, 66–96, 102, 106, 109, 116, 122–133,
    139–142, 154, 156, 164, 170–174, 179, 184
ActiveX controls   83
add-ons   77, 89, 139–141
    Research add-on   89
browsing history   20, 77, 179
browsing tips   74–75
clearing the cache   77
connecting an unsecured PC   66
https   83
Internet Protection Mode   68, 80
padlock icon   75, 78
temporary Internet files   77
zones
    "Internet" zone   80, 82
    "Local intranet" zone   81
    resetting to default   84
    "Restricted sites" zone   80, 83–84
    "Trusted sites" zone   82
Internet chat rooms   52, 74

Internet Explorer   58, 68, 75–78, 80–89, 95, 116,
        124–127, 130–131, 133, 139–142, 171–173, 179
    advanced settings   85
    auto-complete, turning off   88
    cookies   88
    information bar   87
    pop-up blocker   86
    security settings   80
    zones   80, 82, 84, 116
IP addresses   94, 108, 127–132
    private and public   127
    range   128, 132
    static   127–128, 131
        setting   128

J

Junk email   11, 98, 106, 109, 111
    bouncing   109
    deterring   108
    identifying   106
    intentional spelling errors   107, 118
    IP address used   108
    Junk E-mail Filter   110
        Blocked Senders List   114–115
        Junk E-mail Options   113–115
        protection levels   110–112
        Safe Senders List   105, 111–114
    message boards   108
    most common subjects   107
    pump and dump schemes   107
    random subject header   107
    spoofed addresses   107, 109
    Unsolicited Bulk Email (UBE), defined   106
    Unsolicited Commercial Email (UCE), defined 106

K

Kensington security slot   23
    padlock logo   23
Keystroke capture   14, 66–67

L

License agreements   73

M

Macros   61, 165–166, 168
    checking settings   165
MAC address   127, 130, 133–134
    filtering by   133–134
Mailwasher   109, 118
Malware   10, 12, 35, 38, 51, 66–70,
        73, 79, 90, 143, 158–159, 165, 170, 184
Message boards   26, 108, 170, 176, 184
Microsoft Management Console (MMC) 48, 137, 186
    snap-ins   48, 89, 137, 186
Microsoft SpyNet   70, 72
Microsoft TechNet   170, 173
Microsoft Website   171
    Knowledge Base   172
Modems   9, 59, 66, 79, 123
MS-DOS   179

N

Network Access Protection   15
Network adapter   133
Network security   26, 122–134
    dial-up   22, 59, 66–67, 79, 123
    firewalls   68, 75,
        90, 92–94, 108, 123–124, 130–132, 164, 186
        preventing access by time   131
        rules   131
        ZoneAlarm   130
    modems   59, 66, 79, 123
    routers   123–128, 130–133
        password-protecting   124
        web browser interface   124
    wireless networks 14, 91, 122–127, 129–131, 134
        pre-shared key   126
        WEP security key   125–126
        WPA security key   125–126

Network Tools 13
  ping 13, 93, 124
Newsgroups 174–176
  creating a new post 176
  etiquette 176
  news server 174–175
  posting messages 175–176
  replying to a post 176

O

Online banking 18–20, 66, 74–76, 78, 82, 88
Over-the-shoulder credentials 15, 38, 51

P

Parental Controls 15, 52–54
  adult content 52
  age-inappropriate games 52
  blocking inappropriate content 54
  Internet chat rooms 52
  setting time limits 53
Passphrase 125–126
Passwords 12–14,
  16, 26–30, 34, 43–44, 67, 74, 88, 126, 167
  changing 44
  complexity 30, 34, 124, 126, 136
  cracking 14
    brute-force attack 14
    dictionary attack 14, 28
  password hint warning 43
  setting 43
  strength 28
  strong passwords 28–30, 167
  weak passwords 28
Patches 185
PayPal 12, 103

PC security
  cost of 8
  history 9, 18
  layered approach 15, 21
  mission-critical computing 22
  online security tests 95
    ShieldsUP! 95–96, 122
  relation to home security 8, 16, 19
  security strategy 16, 32, 39
  stealth mode 96
  the trade-off 85, 87
  value of stored data 18
Peer-to-peer file-sharing programs 62, 67, 74
Permissions 45–47
  full control 46
  inherited 46
  list folder contents 46
  modify 46
  read 46
  read and execute 46
  write 46
Phishing 12–13,
  15, 67–68, 74, 76, 98–106, 109–110, 184
  fisherman analogy 99
  live example 99
  mode of operation 76
  reporting phishing attempts 103
    eBay 103
  scare tactics 100
  unblocking legitimate messages 105
  website detection 68
Phishing filter 15, 76, 104–106
Physical PC security 9, 18–24
  alarms 23
  cages 21
  drive locks 22
  enclosures 22
  invisible ink 24
  lockers 23
  security cables 20, 23
  stamping 24
  thinking like a criminal 24
  tracking devices 22
Piggybacking 14, 123
Ping 13
Pop-ups 11, 86–87, 155
Pop-up Blocker 86
  adding exceptions 87
  allowed-sites list 87
  filter level 87
  pop-unders 86
  pop-up hell 86
Public folder 39, 47, 91–92, 127, 156, 167

R

Real time protection   60, 70–71, 73
Remote-control tools   13
   Back Orifice   13
   NetBus   13
Remote Desktop   50, 160
   disabling   160
Retiring a PC   178
Rogue dialers   66, 79, 86, 123
   premium-rate phone lines   67
Rootkits   12, 66, 184

S

Secure Socket Layer (SSL)   78, 83
Security by obscurity   129
Security Center   158
Services
   described   159
   disabling   159
Service Packs   185
Social engineering   12–13, 28
Softpedia verification service   69
Sophos website   57
Spam   11, 16, 56, 103, 106, 110, 120, 184
   spammers   106–109, 115, 118–119, 175
   unsubscribe options   11, 108
Spyware   10–11, 58, 66–74,
   76, 79, 108, 143, 158–159, 170, 184, 186
   antispyware 69–70, 73, 79, 108, 158, 164, 170, 186
      AdAware   69, 73
      alternatives   69, 73
      Microsoft SpyNet   70, 72
      Spybot Search & Destroy   73
      Windows Defender   15, 68, 70–73
Storage   24, 144, 181
   software media   24
Symantec website   14

T

Transport Layer Security (TLS)   78, 83

U

USB flash drives   26, 60, 62, 143–144, 148
User accounts   38, 40, 48, 50
   groups   48–49, 50
      Administrators group   49
      Remote Desktop users group   50
      users group   48, 50
   Guest   39, 42
   naming convention   41
   new Vista model   167
   setting a password   43
User Account Control 15, 30, 38, 40, 43, 48, 51, 59, 62,
   91–94, 129, 138, 150, 159–160, 164, 180, 186
User community   170

V

Viruses   9–10, 14, 56–64, 66–67, 98, 184
   ambiguity   56
   antivirus software   58–60
      Avast!   58–60, 62, 158
      McAfee   63
      virus definitions   61–62
   becoming more powerful   10
   Bin-Laden virus   64
   biological comparison   10, 56
   Brain virus   57
   defined   56
   hoaxes   63
      "a virtual card for you" hoax   63
      Budweiser screensaver hoax   63
      hoax database   63
      jdbgmgr.exe hoax   64
      Olympic Torch hoax   64
   infection indications   61
   in the wild   57
   libraries   57
   macros   61
   MyDoom virus   10

Trojan horses   10–11, 14, 56–58, 70, 74, 98, 184
   Backdoor.Haxdoor   14
Trust Center   61, 165–166

payload   10, 56, 64
scanning for   60
  archive files   60

W

War driving   14, 123
Web chat   54
Windows
  patches   98, 185
  Vista   8, 15, 30, 38, 40, 42, 44, 47– 48,
        51–52, 54, 68, 70, 76, 90, 92, 102, 104,
        110–111, 122, 130, 136–137, 139, 141, 149,
        154–155, 158–160, 167, 173, 179–180, 186
    additional security   158
    security model   15
  Windows 3.1   9
  Windows 95   9
Windows Defender   15, 68, 70–73
  definitions files   70
  quarantined items   72
  real time defense   70
  scanning   70–71
  software explorer   72
  SpyNet   70, 72
  tools   72
Windows Explorer   74, 139, 155, 161–162
  Folder Options   161–162
    hidden files and folders   161
    hiding known file extensions   161
    hiding protected operating system files   161
Windows Firewall   15, 68, 90–94, 124, 130
  allowing ICMP traffic   93
  block all incoming connections   91
  building and construction analogy   90
  exceptions   92
  security log   94
Windows Mail 80, 98–99, 101–120, 156, 174–176
  blocking images   102, 116–117
  Junk email filter   110
  "Junk E-mail" folder   101, 104, 106, 110–111
  message rules   108, 118
    action to be taken   119
    conditions   118
    naming your rule   119
    testing   120
  more security options   116
Windows Update   70, 185

Worms   10, 14, 56–58, 67, 70, 74, 98, 184
  Blaster worm   61
  Spida worm   27–28

Z

Zombie PC   12, 67, 106, 108, 184